Coming of Age in Reference Services: A Case History of the Washington State University Libraries

Coming of Age in Reference Services: A Case History of the Washington State University Library has been co-published simultaneously as *The Reference Librarian*, Number 64 1999.

Coming of Age
in Reference Services:
A Case History
of the Washington State
University Libraries

Christy Zlatos
Editor

Coming of Age in Reference Services: A Case History of the Washington State University Libraries has been co-published simultaneously as *The Reference Librarian*, Number 64 1999.

Routledge
Taylor & Francis Group

NEW YORK AND LONDON

Coming of Age in Reference Services: A Case History of the Washington State University Libraries has been co-published simultaneously as *The Reference Librarian*, Number 64 1999.

The development, preparation, and publication of this work has been undertaken with great care. However, the publisher, employees, editors, and agents of The Haworth Press and all imprints of The Haworth Press, Inc., including The Haworth Medical Press® and Pharmaceutical Products Press®, are not responsible for any errors contained herein or for consequences that may ensue from use of materials or information contained in this work. Opinions expressed by the author(s) are not necessarily those of The Haworth Press, Inc.

First published 1999 by The Haworth Press, Inc.
10 Alice Street, Binghamton, NY 13904-1580 USA ı, NY 13904-1580 USA

This edition published 2013 by Routledge

Routledge   Routledge
Taylor & Francis Group   Taylor & Francis Group
711 Third Avenue   2 Park Square Milton Park,
New York, NY 10017, USA   Abingdon Oxfordshire OX14 4RN

First issued in paperback 2016

Routledge is an imprint of the Taylor & Francis Group, an informa business

Cover design by Thomas J. Mayshock Jr.

Library of Congress Cataloging-in-Publication Data

Coming of age in reference services: a case history of the Washington State University Libraries/ Christy Zlatos, editor.
     p. cm.
     "Co-published simultaneously as The reference librarian, number 64, 1999."
     Includes bibliographical references and index.
     ISBN 0-7890-0666-9 (alk. paper)
     1. Washington State University. Libraries. 2. Academic libraries–Reference services– Washington, (State)–Pullman. 3. Academic libraries–Reference services–United States Case studies. I. Zlatos, Christy. II. Reference librarian.
Z733.W393C66 1999
027.7'0979739–dc21   99-26012
                                                            CIP

ISBN 13: 978-1-138-97113-4 (pbk)
ISBN 13: 978-0-7890-0666-0 (hbk)

Coming of Age in Reference Services: A Case History of the Washington State University Libraries

CONTENTS

ABOUT THE EDITOR

Christy Zlatos, MSLS, is Head of Media Materials Services at Washington State University at Pullman. She has held positions at Northeastern University, Auburn University, and University of Southern Indiana as a reference librarian. Currently, Ms. Zlatos is book review co-editor of the *Journal of Academic Librarianship*.

Introduction and Dedication

This volume is a celebration of the perseverance, ingenuity, and talent of the librarians who have served, past and present, at the Holland Library reference desk. It is also dedicated to Pauline Lilje, our retired colleague and friend, who staffed the reference desk in various capacities from 1967 until she retired in 1996.

Nearly every librarian presently employed at the reference desk participated in this project and most contributed an article. The assignment was simple. Write about that aspect of Holland reference that especially interests you. Characterize it. Capture its spirit. What is it about what you do within Holland Reference that you might want to tell your colleagues?

Much of the writing within this volume reflects a local, day-to-day concern rather than an attempt to solve the problems within our discipline or to project what reference services will be like in the 21st century. Readers who hope to easily answer the question, "How have Holland Reference Services responded to the demands of constant change?"(and then dismiss us), may find that easy answers to the question elude them. Certainly we have changed, and we respond to an environment of constant changes every day. But within Holland Reference Services, with its participatory management based on consensus, the changes are often subtle and slow in coming. They are also not always readily apparent.

Taken together, the following articles characterize the many-faceted Holland Reference Services for readers. Certainly our triumphs are showcased (can't fault us that), but then so are our ideas, our trials, and our difficulties. Writing about what one most intimately associates as work has been wickedly simple for some of us but desperately chal-

[Haworth co-indexing entry note]: "Introduction and Dedication." Zlatos, Christy. Co-published simultaneously in *The Reference Librarian* (The Haworth Press, Inc.) No. 64, 1999, pp. 1-8; and: *Coming of Age in Reference Services: A Case History of the Washington State University Libraries* (ed: Christy Zlatos) The Haworth Press, Inc., 1999, pp. 1-8. Single or multiple copies of this article are available for a fee from The Haworth Document Delivery Service [1-800-342-9678, 9:00 a.m. - 5:00 p.m. (EST). E-mail address: getinfo@haworthpressinc.com].

lenging for others. For the latter group, who faced the writing as a challenge, the topics came quickly, but then projects faltered as authors discovered that their holy wars demanded detailed explanation. Others discovered that their fingers must come out of the dikes (at least temporarily) of those same problems that they had been holding firm for years in order to describe them for the readers.

COMING OF AGE IN REFERENCE SERVICES

The title of the volume, *Coming of Age in Reference Services* is, of course, a play on the title of Margaret Mead's 1929 classic, *Coming of Age in Samoa*. However, instead of writing "a psychological study of primitive youth for Western Civilization,"[1] as Mead did, the writing in this volume focuses upon library colleagues coming of age as academic reference librarians, library educators, technology and Web designers, administrators, and as writers.

To understand an anthropological approach, reading the Foreword of *Coming of Age* by Franz Boas is useful. In it Boas writes:

> And yet the way in which the personality reacts to culture is a matter that should concern us deeply and that makes the studies of foreign cultures a fruitful and useful field of research. We are accustomed to consider all those actions that are part and parcel of our own culture, standards which we follow automatically as common to all mankind. They are deeply ingrained in our behaviour. We are moulded in their forms so that we cannot think but that they must be valid everywhere.[2]

Certainly the tools of the academic library workplace, the reference books, hardware and software, and databases that we all use with regularity, are part and parcel of our own culture. But, in this *Coming of Age,* the authors have tried to capture and characterize for the readers what is unique to Holland Reference Services. To read about

---

1. Quotation is from Mead's subtitle. See Mead, Margaret, *Coming of Age in Samoa: A Psychological Study of Primitive Youth for Western Civilization.* (London: Jonathan Cape, 1929). (My edition is British; the American edition was published in 1928.)
2. Ibid., xiv.

another's culture in the workplace and to approach an understanding of it is to gain a better insight into one's own.

OUR GREYING PROFILE

Stanley Wilder's study of the demographic patterns of librarians in ARL libraries that notes and comments on the profession's greying profile in relation to adapting to an electronic information environment and planning for future library services,[3] brings up the question, how "grey" are the librarian authors who have written articles within these pages? Wilder's profile does seem to sum up the Holland reference librarians rather well. The largest group of our librarians would describe themselves as "midcareer," with perhaps some beginning to approach retirement age in 5-10 years; a smaller group of colleagues in their 20s and 30s also exists.

THE "COMING OF AGE" ARTICLES

Within this volume the articles stand center stage as a testament to the diverse interests of the Holland reference librarians. That none of our authors chose to write about the actual reference service performed so ably could be taken as significant; also absent are specific articles dealing with one of our traditional duties, collection development. However, readers will find articles on topics from training and retraining reference professionals to an examination of the Generation X in our midst.

In honor of Pauline Lilje, two articles have been written which offer some insight into Holland Public Services' roots in the 1978 "merger" of two divisional libraries, the Humanities Library and the Social Sciences Library.

We take great pride in our user education programs at Washington State University; this volume contains two articles on user education

---

3. Although Wilder wrote a report, *The Age Demographics of Academic Librarians: A Profession Apart,* published by ARL, my information comes from a nice, short treatment of the topic. See Wilder, Stanley, "Generational Change and the Niche for Librarians," *Journal of Academic Librarianship* 22 (September 1996): 385-6.

topics. The first is from two librarians relatively new to our staff and suggests a new and basic approach to English 101 and beyond; the second is a discussion of the coming of age of our nationally-recognized General Education course with a library component, the World Civilizations project.

International librarianship, a field that has involved many WSU librarians abroad in various projects, is represented here with an article by our 1996 Library Fellow, who discusses her experience in libraries both in the United States and in her native Lithuania.

This volume, further, offers three articles about the management of the technology in Holland Reference Services. The first, about electronic resource librarians (ERLs), demonstrates how four Holland reference librarian positions have been adapted to cover the management and maintenance of the many electronic resources in the department. The many duties covered include computer troubleshooting, managing CD-ROMs, GIS, and the Libraries' Home Pages, teaching classes in the use of technology, and other computer-related duties. The second and third articles, also by electronic resource librarians or former electronic resource librarians, cover both the management of CD-ROM and electronic document sources and the management of GIS services at Washington State University.

THE LOCAL CONTEXT IN THE APPENDICES

To provide readers with a context in which to place our Holland Reference Services, two appendices have been provided by the editor of the volume. Some miscellaneous characteristics of the Holland Reference Services have been gathered into an appendix titled "About Washington State University Libraries' Holland Reference Services." To acquaint readers with a sense of our scale, something of our direction and our interests, "A Chronology of the History of Washington State University Libraries" has been prepared.

ABOUT PAULINE LILJE

With her bachelor's degree in Art and her MFA (majoring in sculpture) in hand, Pauline Lilje landed at the University of Illinois in 1962.

But, she could only find a temporary teaching position in the Department of Fine Arts to do sculpture because universities in those antique days did not often hire women in full-time, tenure-track positions. In her own words from her resume, at that time it made "economic sense to avail herself of the opportunity to attend library school as a research assistant in civil engineering." During the years 1964-67, Lilje attended the Illinois library school, graduating except-for-the-language-requirement, A.B.D.

Lilje arrived at Washington State University in 1967 and was hired at the library by University Librarian G. Donald Smith. Over the years, she served in a variety of capacities with social sciences and humanities reference, including Chief of Social Science Library from July 1974 through January 1978 (resigning as Chief because a new director was "heading in directions she could not follow.").

Again, from her resume in her own words, her assignments were "(1) the provision of information resources and reference services in all Humanities and Social Sciences subject areas to all library patrons, and (2) collection development related to [her] subject background in art."

Known for her candor, her boundless enthusiasm, and a joyful approach to the reference interview with undergraduates, when at work Pauline Lilje enjoyed the people at the reference desk as much as she enjoyed working with the beginning librarians in Holland reference. Although she retired in 1996 and now lives and pursues art in Portland, Oregon, with her husband, Gerry, we miss her. We are grateful that she touched our lives.

* * *

I remember the first time I ever saw Pauline. The image I still see is the tattooed arms, long flowing gray hair, braless, wearing a sleeveless tank top shell with beaded necklace and earrings, slacks and wedgies. I always knew exactly when she would walk past my desk in Old Holland as I could hear her coming down the hall—the distinct sound of her beaded necklace and earrings moving as she walked. Pauline beaded necklaces and long matching earrings for every outfit. She went through many clothing style changes while I worked with her. After she moved into the shoe comfort zone and began to wear Birkenstocks, she still made sure she matched—she dyed her socks to go with her tops. I miss Pauline. I miss seeing her beautiful art work, listening to her tell stories of her life before and after the library, the talks we'd have about anything and everything, reading her one-of-a-kind handwriting with the skinny, inch-tall letters, her "unforgettable memos," us griping about the smell of her Kimchee lunches, the many times she brought chips, cheese and bean dip or veggies with her homemade horseradish dip that she called "A Sort of Recipe." Pauline kept the Reference Work Area lively. She was often outspoken and didn't care who heard her. That is one reason she is truly one-of-a-kind, and I miss her very much.

Kathy McGreevy
Library Secretary

I enjoyed sitting with Pauline in her garden or her kitchen (drinking Pink Zin) and discussing something like faculty status but what I really remember is one day in the old Holland reference section when Pauline told me she was from Detroit where one important thing folks on the automobile assembly lines learn is that the management regularly steps up the tempo to make the workers work harder. The workers with their noses to the grindstone don't understand how hard they are working or that they are being exploited. I answered "Uh-huh," but I didn't really understand. The truth was I genuinely was puzzled because I believed that the management had little knowledge of what the workers at WSU Libraries did. Libraries' workers, especially the faculty, seemed self-motivated. It was only after it dawned on me that the equation of stepping up the tempo didn't need a "who" to be valid that the power of Pauline's statement became clear to me. A young, library faculty person's enthusiastic "stepping up of the tempo" could become deadly if she didn't learn some restraint and self-management techniques. I am still learning.

Christy Zlatos

I feel very fortunate to have had the opportunity to work with Pauline. Always a free spirit, Pauline provided me with stories from the past, insights into the library profession, new ideas, and the challenge to keep up with her creative endeavors. When I think of Pauline now, the colorful barn owl eyes and strange surreal creatures of her beadwork come to mind. Pauline is hip. She could always find a way to tie my interest in new technology to images and myths of the past. It was always fun to pop into Pauline's office and get her take on whatever topic was on her mind at the time. She was never hesitant to shock people, or stir things up a little. I miss Pauline, and will never forget all the things she taught me–especially that KWIC stands for "key word in context."

Jane Scales

Pauline has the sense of humor that is borne of intelligence, the imagination which comes from quickness of mind. To extol of her free-spirited, creative style paints only part of the portrait. A tribute should mention her intellect, and her insight derived from education and experience. Not only was she well-liked, but respected as a librarian who knew her stuff. She may be the only librarian on the planet who ever had concurrent responsibilities for collections in Fine Arts, Architecture, Design–and Law. She has that broad background, so appropriate to librarianship, which encompasses many varied interests, a desire to learn, and to relate.

With a visual memory that delighted some and confounded others, Pauline could describe with equal authority the inner workings of Lexis-Nexis, the style of a Fortuny skirt, the workflow of book-processing, a Bach fugue or a horse race. I remember her references to Man Ray, to Kant, to some baseball star I'd never heard of, and I miss her art of old-fashioned conversation, the kind of stimulating, knowledge-based conversation you have to have read books to contribute to, and have had a love affair with experience to make interesting.

She was generous with professional and personal wisdom, some of which may have eluded me at the time but is much valued now. Her sensible, informed tips-are still coming my way, welcomed with gratitude, as I continue in my career. To have known her, to know her today, is a privilege of my life at WSU.

Paula Elliot

Having written it all at this point, we will say no more.

Christy Zlatos

Training and Retraining Reference Professionals: Core Competencies for the 21st Century

Mary M. Nofsinger

SUMMARY. In the academic reference environment transformed by electronic technologies, budgetary constraints, and a vast array of new information resources, the author maintains that reference librarians need training and retraining in the following core competencies: reference skills and subject knowledge, communication and interpersonal abilities, technological skills and knowledge, analytic and critical thinking skills, supervisory and management skills, and commitment to user services. The author considers each core competency in the context of the most important factors responsible for continuing changes in the training and retraining of reference professionals. Although responsibility for providing continuing education opportunities resides with library managers, in the end, each reference librarian must assume responsibility for acquiring new knowledge and developing new skills. As librarianship moves towards the 21st century, librarians must educate themselves to survive in the evolving Information Society. *[Article copies available for a fee from The Haworth Document Delivery Service: 1-800-342-9678. E-mail address: getinfo@haworthpressinc.com]*

In the past twenty years, academic libraries have been transformed by electronic technologies, budgetary constraints, and a vast array of new information resources. Despite drastic changes in work environ-

Mary M. Nofsinger is Former Head of Reference, Holland/New Library, Room 120J, Pullman, WA 99164-5610 (E-mail: mnofsing@wsu.edu).

[Haworth co-indexing entry note]: "Training and Retraining Reference Professionals: Core Competencies for the 21st Century." Nofsinger, Mary M. Co-published simultaneously in *The Reference Librarian* (The Haworth Press, Inc.) No. 64, 1999, pp. 9-19; and: *Coming of Age in Reference Services: A Case History of the Washington State University Libraries* (ed: Christy Zlatos) The Haworth Press, Inc., 1999, pp. 9-19. Single or multiple copies of this article are available for a fee from The Haworth Document Delivery Service [1-800-342-9678, 9:00 a.m. - 5:00 p.m. (EST). E-mail address: getinfo@haworthpressinc.com].

ments, increased job responsibilities, and new role expectations, reference librarians still need training in the following core competencies:
reference skills and subject knowledge, communication and interpersonal abilities, technological skills and knowledge, analytic and critical thinking skills, supervisory and managerial skills, and commitment
to user services. This article will discuss the most important factors
responsible for continuing changes in the training and retraining of
reference professionals.

THE CHANGING ENVIRONMENT

In the 1980s the normal paradigm of academic librarianship involved
reference interview techniques (e.g., question negotiation), information
assistance utilizing print resources primarily, collection development by
librarian subject specialists, user instruction, and occasional librarian-
mediated on-line searching via DIALOG or other commercial vendors.
In many libraries, microfilm and typewriters were the most advanced
technologies. Users' access to library resources was predominately via
card catalogs and printed indexes to periodical literature. In addition,
academic libraries heavily emphasized the purchase and conservation
of library materials needed by primary clientele which included faculty, staff, and students in the local community.

By the mid-1990s, academic librarians have assimilated additional
duties, knowledge and skills, particularly in regard to microcomputers
and automation. In addition to providing the traditional informational
services mentioned earlier, reference librarians have become technological experts at assessing on-line OPACs, CD-ROM products with
differing search protocols, electronic mail, Internet resources, full-text
databases, LANs, and national networks. As a result of these technological advances, the sheer volume of available information has greatly increased at the same time that economic restrictions have forced
downsizing and restructuring in many academic libraries.

REFERENCE SKILLS AND SUBJECT KNOWLEDGE

During the "good old days" in the 1980s, prior to major technological developments, the training of academic reference professionals

was considerably easier and simpler. Numerous articles in the library literature provide an overview of reference training techniques.[1] In general, the Head of Reference planned and coordinated a phased sequence of learning opportunities which involved an orientation to reference and other departments within the Library and meetings with subject specialist librarians for training in specific areas of reference and collection development. Opportunities for examination of a core collection of reference sources were provided, and each new professional was expected to develop expertise in using the core collection. In addition, librarians were expected to observe transactions at the reference desk and to gain ample on-the-job experience with colleagues acting as mentors.

As the reference environment changed in the 1990s, the roles of reference librarians also changed from conservators, collectors, and resource caretakers. At present, reference librarians have become information counselors, mediators between users and materials, and educators in response to availability of technology and the need for greater expertise in assisting students and faculty, both within and outside the library walls. Reference service still consists of personal assistance to users, but there is much more emphasis on teaching and guiding users in the pursuit of information. "Libraries are moving further away from the warehouse philosophy towards an access and client-centered approach. The availability of remote electronic access to information means fewer people need to come to the library . . ."[2] but they still need extensive assistance in locating relevant resources. This role shift has led to even heavier workloads and to expanded, more diversified responsibilities for reference librarians.

Current reference skills training focuses on development of ". . . a working knowledge of standard print and electronic sources or specific discipline knowledge . . ."[3] in order to quickly locate and retrieve requested information, regardless of format, wherever it is available. Another complicating factor is that ". . . a number of traditional sources do not have computerized counterparts and the reference librarian will have to convey this to the user who insists on using computers for everything. If a computer counterpart does exist, the reference librarian must know if there are format differences between the two and decide which one is most suitable to the question."[4] Thus, reference queries often take longer to answer due to the various formats and the need for more individualized instruction for users. In summary, it is much more difficult to perform satisfactory reference in the 1990s than in earlier decades.

COMMUNICATION AND INTERPERSONAL SKILLS

Communication skills, both oral and written, have always been essential for good reference librarianship. These skills are even more critical in an automated environment than in the traditional print environment where one could browse without revealing poor spelling skills. When using electronic databases and networks, spelling errors can negatively impact the librarian's success rate in locating information. As Virginia Massey-Burzio points out, "the ability to communicate effectively is becoming increasingly important as academic librarians position themselves to play a more active role in academic life . . . Methods of library instruction will undoubtedly continue to evolve, and will likely place additional demands on our oral communication skills . . . In addition to verbal skills, writing skills are also needed since a considerable part of a reference librarian's life is spent preparing brochures, pathfinders, flyers, point-of-use instruction guides, grant proposals, articles in the campus newspaper and in library newsletters, and other written communication."[5]

Likewise, interpersonal and human relations are even more essential in an automated environment where the reference librarian must deal with users who may be resistant to using electronic resources. In addition, reference librarians must strive to develop new reservoirs of patience, tact, flexibility, and the ability to juggle a variety of questions without alienating the questioners. During the training program, the Head of Reference emphasizes the importance of reference skills used in querying users to determine their informational needs, as well as specific behaviors such as approachability, accuracy, courtesy, and promptness. According to Debbie Kalvee, there is a basic set of communication behaviors which strongly influences quality reference performance: "These behaviors include being friendly and nonjudgmental, asking open questions, verifying a patron's specific question, asking a follow-up question, paraphrasing and paying full attention to the patron. With follow-up coaching and positive reinforcement back on the job, the training program has been shown to truly change behaviors."[6]

In summary, the academic library environment continues to change rapidly in the 1990s, and reference librarians will continue to be challenged to function effectively. Personal flexibility will be an essential interpersonal skill as work routines and job requirements shift. According to Johannah Sherrer, "the personal attributes of librarians have a direct bearing on how effectively individual libraries move forward in providing improved, enhanced and user respected services. In any job or profession, success depends as much on attitude and approach to work as it does on training, knowledge, or appropriate degrees."[7]

TECHNOLOGICAL SKILLS

Back in the early 1980s, reference training programs did not involve many technological skills since only a few electronic resources were available in academic libraries. By the 1990s, however, libraries experienced a phenomenal explosion of technological advances: remote libraries and databases may now be connected using the local online catalog or university computer as a gateway, full-text articles and books are accessible, hundreds of Internet and World Wide Web resources appear daily, electronic publishing and electronic journals are expanding, and virtual library systems[8] incorporate direct access to CD-ROM systems, document delivery, images, abstracts, bibliographic indexes, and worldwide knowledge sources.

According to Michael Malinconico, electronic technologies radically transformed the academic library workplace, changing the services libraries provide, the manner in which these services are delivered, how libraries operate, and the work library employees do.[9] In regard to reference training, it is no longer possible to train librarians once and then expect them to provide ongoing satisfactory service to users. Instead, librarians must be trained and re-trained, again and again, as technologies change and new electronic resources become available. The breadth of training must include microcomputer skills (including knowledge of hardware and software), the ability to read and comprehend technical manuals, the selection of appropriate equipment and software, and knowledge of many different information systems.

Reference training must also ensure that librarians assume the role of consultant and teacher as they show users how to operate a variety of automated tools, from OPACs and CD-ROMs to full-text data files and web browsers. Thus, librarians will need to master intricate features of databases, database access systems, and systems for manipulating data, as well as keep up with new supplements, new software releases, and new information services. In addition, reference librarians must also maintain familiarity with available Internet sources. According to Don Lanier and Walter Wilkins, ". . . it is impossible to maintain state-of-the-art competence without a disciplined effort to routinely navigate the Internet and to interact with colleagues who are also attempting to stay current."[10] In order to develop this level of expertise, librarians must allocate adequate time to study, explore, and maintain their electronic skills–despite other responsibilities.

Cecilia Stafford and William Serban suggest three levels of technological training and expertise for reference librarians:[11] (1) Librarians with basic computer skills and versatility with a number of electronic systems. These librarians have the ability to orient users to basic computer systems but they cannot provide in-depth explanations or troubleshoot. (2) Librarians who are expert in a single system or systems, e.g., a CD-ROM specialist, a CAI developer, a web-master with HTML and WWW home page expertise, etc. These librarians develop a high degree of specialization as "in-house" experts. (3) Information systems librarians who are microcomputer applications specialists with substantial proficiency in all phases of automated reference sources. Library managers need to determine desirable levels of electronic expertise for reference librarians and then provide appropriate continuing education opportunities. Although technostress[12] from continual change cannot be banished from libraries, it can be greatly diminished by providing adequate technological training.

ANALYTIC AND CRITICAL THINKING SKILLS

One of the most valuable skills a reference librarian can develop is the ability to think critically during a reference transaction or query. In the process of determining users' informational needs, a reference librarian needs to ". . . break down queries into manageable, logical parts and. . . forge connections simultaneously with the subject itself and the organization and distribution of resource tools in that field. This ability is enhanced by experience and time in the field and when it is effectively blended with spontaneity and the willingness to abandon prescribed structure, one has the necessary problem solving skills needed for effective reference work."[13] Thus, ". . . the librarian should make informed choices among information sources based on analysis of individual needs and a critical knowledge of reference sources."[14]

However, the reference librarian must not only be able to find relevant information or documents, but must be able to evaluate them on the criteria of availability, ease of access, authority, presence of biases, scope, and timeliness–regardless of electronic or print format or location. In addition, a critical thinking librarian must estimate the quantity and intellectual level of information required by the user. This is particularly true in regard to Internet resources, since "it is important now to be carried away by the momentum of technology and risk overwhelming the user with a vast and varied number of resources . . . By mediating, selecting, and recommending resources, librarians are able to keep users from being swamped by too many documents."[15] With vast quantities of information now available electronically (the so-called "library without walls") and the fluidity of software and databases, there will be ample opportunities for critical thinking librarians to assist users, regardless of their physical proximity.

MANAGEMENT AND SUPERVISORY SKILLS

In prior decades, reference librarians generally focused on developing personal knowledge and expertise in traditional areas, and few ventured into the realm of management. With the proliferation of electronic resources, however, classified staff and student employees have taken over many clerical responsibilities, thereby freeing up librarians to do more professional work, including coordinating activities and supervisory activities. At the same time, academic libraries have created new paraprofessional positions for highly educated professionals without library degrees, particularly in the areas of microcomputers, systems, and automated services. Out of necessity, more librarians have become involved in the management aspects of new technologies, personnel issues, fund-raising, and public relations.

As reference librarians become more involved in strategic planning and the management of library resources, they often need additional training in organizational behavior, conflict resolution, employee motivation, collective bargaining, marketing technologies, and customer relations. They may also need to learn new skills in the areas of licensing agreements, hardware and software documentation, collection of user fees, dealing with database vendors, organizing new training programs for users and staff, scheduling, budgeting, evaluating performance, and marketing services. These skills and knowledge, which must be learned today via continuing professional development activities (courses and workshops, reading library literature, learning from colleagues, etc.), will also be important for successful reference librarians in the twenty-first century.

COMMITMENT TO USER SERVICES

According to Christopher Millson-Martula and Vanaja Menon, "the continued success of a service organization such as an academic library depends upon the organization's ability to adjust its products and services to correspond to user needs."[16] While this may have been true in prior decades, focusing on users' needs has become even more essential in the 1990s due to academic library downsizing and the shift from physical ownership of resources to electronic access (the "just in case" and "just in time" concept) and the evolving virtual library. The quality of user service is largely determined by library employees or computer screens, where users interact with library services and resources. In summary, "the perceived worth and overall success of libraries are in the hand of front line library personnel as they interact with library users, formulate service policies, and design service parameters."[17]

Thus, academic reference librarians play a vital role in influencing users' expectations and satisfaction levels during their direct contacts at the reference desk and through departmental liaison and teaching activities. Successful reference librarians need to be tenacious when querying users, creative at locating requested information, dependable at providing promised services, honest about time-frames for delivery of resources, and forthright about what they can and cannot do. Milson-Martula and Menon describe additional strategies for enhanced librarian communication with users, including:[18]

- serving as essential conduits for information, such as compliments, complaints, concerns, needs, etc., between library managers and customers;
- engaging in market research activity to identify customer needs and expectations, using focus groups, interviews, questionnaires, logs, etc.;

- analyzing customer complaints to improve service delivery processes;
- using survey instruments to obtain customer and staff input;
- creating customer panels representing segments of customers based upon their differing needs and situations; and finally,
- maintaining daily direct contact with changing segments of the library's customer population by improving listening and general communication skills.

In addition, Janet Brown states that reference librarians want to do more than just make their customers happy. "In academic libraries, especially, we want the library to become an integral part of the education process for all students. We want to reach them and teach them how to become independent learners in the library."[19] She discusses more strategies for enhancing user service, including: (1) development of a problem log at the reference desk for problems and complaints; (2) soliciting user feedback via a Suggestion Box, with responses posted nearby on a bulletin board; (3) using an obtrusive survey instrument to gather information about customers and their needs; and (4) developing a reference automation quality circle to address librarian problems related to technological expansion. These activities demonstrate the importance of empowering reference librarians to address user service issues proactively and the benefits of focusing on improving public services.

CONCLUSION:
THE FUTURE

As librarianship moves into the 21st century, "the greatest challenge that faces academic and research libraries, librarians, and staff is the ability to function effectively in a changing environment."[20] In order to cope with rapid technological and societal changes, reference librarians need excellent communication skills, a strong public services orientation, and extensive training and retraining. Knowledge, skills, and attitudes must be constantly updated as users make more complex and sophisticated reference requests than in the past, while demanding a higher level of service, accountability, and competence. Although responsibility for providing continuing education opportunities resides with library managers, each reference librarian must assume responsibility for acquiring new knowledge and developing new skills. A professional is personally responsible for keeping current. Ultimately, librarians must educate themselves to survive in the continually evolving Information Society.

NOTES

1. Anne May Berwind, "Orientation for the Reference Desk," RSR: Reference Services Review 19 (Fall 1991): 51-54, 70; Tara Lynn Fulton, "Mentor Meets Telemachus: The Role of the Department Head in Orienting and Inducting the Beginning Reference Librarian," *The Reference Librarian*, no. 30 (1990): 257-73; Lillian M. Rider, "Training Program for Reference Desk Staff," 2nd ed. (Montreal: McLennon Library, McGill University, 1979) ED 175486; Karen Y. Stabler, "The Dynamics of Reference Librarianship," *The Reference Librarian*, no. 30 (1990): 133-143; William F. Young, "Communicating With the New Reference Librarian: The Teaching Process," *The Reference Librarian*, no. 16 (1986): 223-231.

2. Ann de Klerk and Joanne R. Euster, "Technology and Organizational Metamorphoses," *Library Trends* 37, no. 4(Spring 1989): 463.

3. Johannah Sherrer, "Thriving in Changing Times: Competencies for Today's Reference Librarians," *The Roles of Reference Librarians: Today and Tomorrow*, edited by Kathleen Low (New York: The Haworth Press, Inc., 1996) p. 14.

4. Cecilia D. Stafford and William M. Serban, "Core Competencies: Recruiting, Training, and Evaluating in the Automated Reference Environment," *Journal of Library Administration* 13, no. 1/2(1990): 87-88.

5. Virginia Massey-Burzio, "Education and Experience: Or, the MLS is Not Enough," *RSR: Reference Services Review* 19 no. 1(Spring 1991): 72-73.

6. Debbie Kalvee, "Successful Reference Training on a Shoestring," *Library Administration and Management* 10, no. 4(Fall 1996): 210.

7. Sherrer, 1996, p. 16.

8. Laverna M. Saunders, ed., *The Evolving Virtual Library: Visions and Case Studies* (Medford, NJ: Information Today, Inc., 1996).

9. S. Michael Malinconico, "Technology and the Academic Workplace," *Library Administration & Management* 5, no. 1(Winter 1991): 25-28.

10. Don Lanier and Walter Wilkins, "Ready Reference Via the Internet," *RQ* 33, no.3(Spring 1994): 365.

11. Stafford and Serban, 1990, p.90.

12. John Kupersmith, "Technostress and the Reference Librarian," *RSR: Reference Services Review* 20, no. 2(Summer 1992): 7-14, 50.

13. Sherrer, 1996, p.15.

14. Threasa L. Wesley, "The Reference Librarian's Critical Skill: Critical Thinking and Professional Service," *The Reference Librarian*, no. 30(1990): 72.

15. Lanier and Wilkins, 1994, pp. 366-367.

16. Christopher Millson-Martula and Vanaja Menon, "Customer Expectations: Concepts and Reality for Academic Library Services," *College and Research Libraries* 56, no. 1(January 1995): 34.

17. Sherrer, 1996, p. 16.

18. Millson-Martula and Menon, 1995, pp. 43-44.

19. Janet Dagenais Brown, "Using Quality Concepts to Improve Reference Services," *College and Research Libraries* 55, no. 3(May 1994): 214.

20. Susan Jurow, "Preparing Academic and Research Library Staff for the 1990's and Beyond," *Journal of Library Administration* 17(1992): 14.

A Neo-Modern Summary of the Futcha:
An Exploration
of the Generation X in Our Midst

B. Jane Scales

SUMMARY. The author explores the concept of Generation X and re-flects on her experiences as an academic librarian who demographically fits into this generation of individuals born between 1961 and 1981. After a definition of the concept and a review of the literature, the author reveals her own experience as a member of this generation and her initial professional impressions as an academic librarian. A brief discussion of the implications of Generation X on libraries in the future concludes the essay. *[Article copies available for a fee from The Haworth Document Delivery Service: 1-800-342-9678. E-mail address: getinfo@haworthpressinc.com]*

INTRODUCTION

Imagine arriving at a beach at the end of a long summer of wild goings-on. The beach crowd is exhausted, the sand shopworn, hot, and full of debris–no place for walking barefoot. You step on a bottle, and some cop yells at you for littering. The sun is directly overhead and leaves no patch of shade that hasn't already been taken. You feel the glare beating down on a barren landscape devoid of secrets or innocence. You look around at the

B. Jane Scales is Reference Librarian, Slavic Bibliographer, and Electronic Resource Librarian, Holland/New Library, Room 120, Pullman, WA 99164-5610 (E-mail: scales@wsu.edu).

[Haworth co-indexing entry note]: "A Neo-Modern Summary of the Futcha: An Exploration of the Generation X in Our Midst." Scales, B. Jane. Co-published simultaneously in *The Reference Librarian* (The Haworth Press, Inc.) No. 64, 1999, pp. 21-30; and: *Coming of Age in Reference Services: A Case History of the Washington State University Libraries* (ed: Christy Zlatos) The Haworth Press, Inc., 1999, pp. 21-30. Single or multiple copies of this article are available for a fee from The Haworth Document Delivery Service [1-800-342-9678, 9:00 a.m. - 5:00 p.m. (EST). E-mail address: getinfo@haworthpressinc.com].

disapproving faces and can't help but sense that, somehow, the entire universe is gearing up to punish you.[1]

This passage, meant to describe the experiences of the generation that came of age during the 1980s and '90s, is the opening paragraph to Strauss and Howe's *13th Gen: Abort, Retry, Ignore, Fail?*–the book that came to define the popular term "Generation X." In this article, I will explore the concept of Generation X and reflect on my experiences as an academic librarian who demographically fits into the generation that arrived "after it all happened."

BACKGROUND AND EXPLANATION OF "GENERATION X"

Although Strauss and Howe do not refer specifically to the post-boomer generation as "Generation X" in either of their books, *13th Gen*, or *Generations*,[2] works which examine the roles and personalities of the generations in America, they crystallized the popular definition of a generation of individuals born between 1961 and 1981. Douglas Coupland brought the term "Generation X" into fashion with his book of the same title,[3] which recounts the fictional exploits of a group of young adults after college. However, the term "Generation X" reportedly originated in the 1960s, and was later the name of Billy Idol's rock band in the late 1970s.

There have been many other terms and phrases used to describe this generation: "twentysomethings" (popularized by *Time* magazine, August, 1990), "baby-busters," "13th Generation," and "boomerang generation" to name a few. Generation X-ers, pundits purport, share some behavioral and attitudinal tendencies, although it's difficult to pin down exactly which tendencies individuals from this generation share. Strauss and Howe, for example, consider this "13th Generation" an "atomized" generation, in that its members represent a diverse array of opinions and outlooks that cannot be neatly defined.

Published studies and surveys conflict in their depiction of Generation X. Despite the complexity of accurately describing such a diverse group of people, it's not difficult to bring to mind the stereotypes promoted by the self-proclaimed experts and marketers; Generation X (all together now) is an apathetic, cynical technology-driven group. Highly entrepreneurial, they do not readily take to corporate culture.

This group values flexibility in the workplace, and craves information and learning opportunities.

MY EXPERIENCE AND OPINIONS
ABOUT "GENERATION X"

There have been scores of articles, studies, research surveys, and books on the topic of Generation X. I avidly read many of these publications for a while–when the whole concept was new and received a lot of media attention. From an early age, I took an interest in pop-culture. (Scenes from the *Monkees, Banana Splits, Scooby Doo*, and *Sesame Street* form my earliest memories.) In the same respect, Generation X is another example of a popular "pet-rock" creation that followed the traditional pattern of other marketable pop icons: familiarity, commercialization, and saturation (death).

Marketers were quick to latch on to the concept of a "new generation" for which they could conduct demographic studies before they repackaged and sold the same old products. I think they perfected this art in the 1970s.

Another reason, though, that led me to actively read about the topic is the simple fact that I fit into this age-group, and there were a few interesting publications that went beyond the formulaic models presented in market studies. In the late 1980s and early 1990s, it was new and interesting to pick up books and articles read analyses of "your" attitudes and behavior, and studies of how the zeitgeist of the 1970s and 1980s somehow stamped your outlook. It became clear why I had, at the age of eleven, found myself nostalgic for 1960s pop icons that I didn't even remember.[4] The alternative was watching the goofy disco phenomenon take root, and contemplate what Watergate *really* meant.

Even as I proceeded through high school and college, it seemed that everyone measured the current political climate, economic situation, music, and mood of the country against that of the 1960s. For that reason, it was refreshing to see the reference point shift to and reflect the events and decades that I remembered and to which I could relate.

I don't agree one-hundred percent with any one assessment or summary, nor am I even sure of the viability of "Generation X." The whole topic of "generations" is pretty slippery. Where do they begin and end? Are they determined by specific dates, or by shared memories of a peer group? More than anything, I found value in reading material by authors, like Coupland, who recognized the millions of younger adults who did not grow up with the memories and experiences, which for thirty years have been considered the standard American "default." It's from this point of view, that I understand what has become known as "Generation X."

INITIAL PROFESSIONAL IMPRESSIONS

In the early '90s, I earned my MLIS and landed my first professional job at Washington State University. This was a very positive experience for me. I was assigned collection development duties in the areas of my undergraduate and graduate studies, worked on the reference desk, and was fortunate enough to have the freedom to explore and develop expertise in other areas of library services, most notably electronic resources. After one of my colleagues took a sabbatical, I began managing the growing collection of CD-ROMs in the Social Sciences and Humanities subject areas.

After working a little while, it became clear to me that the library environment was changing very rapidly, and that the pace of change was accelerating. My colleagues and I continually encountered challenges brought about by the expanding role of technology, and the shifting demands and expectations this elicited from library users and administrators.

In this environment, it was common to hear discussion reflecting the fact that most of my co-workers had experienced a very different professional life than what I saw unfolding before my eyes. While I found the implementation of umpteen new electronic databases and the possibilities of the Internet exciting, others had a different point of view. To many of them, these innovations reflected a new and growing element of instability and complexity to what had for a long time been a job that, after a certain amount of experience, one could do with relative ease and confidence. Until the late '80s or early '90s, one could be sure that the methods and materials used this month would be the same next month.

The working environment of the 1960s, '70s, and '80s were not only more stable, I gather, but there were also fewer pesky budget problems that seem to dominate every purchase decision we now make. In "those times" libraries had a hard time spending all the money available to them. New purchasing and acquisition systems had to be developed to handle the massive amounts of material being processed and made available in libraries.

I see proof of these generous budgets just by walking through the stacks or searching our online catalog. The percentage of books published in the 1960s and 1970s seem unusually high compared to the more recent purchases, reflecting the buying power of libraries then. Books were cheaper, and tax laws didn't discourage publishers from stocking-up on titles for the more rare purchase request. And, of course, the public and the government was more eager to fund higher-education.

These days, it seems, everything misses the mark. Journal subscriptions are being cut. Collection development allocations are stagnant in the best years. Staff cuts have placed more burden on employees, and business is increasing. New types of resources and access methods require everyone to continually make adjustments and concentrate on the moving target of technology.

GENERATION X IN THE LIBRARIES

During my first two years at Washington State University, I lived in fear that budget cuts would result in my position being eliminated. I wondered if other people who had recently become librarians felt the same worn-beach scenario described in the opening passage of *13th Gen*. If, for a time, my continued employment seemed dubious, the culture of the library did not. It was clear that by the time I got here, all the decisions and traditions concerning everyday operations were firmly in place. If the various practices of the reference desk, collection development, and the library culture were open to explanation, they were not necessarily open to question or change–at least not without a painstaking recount of how and why they got were they are now (and why they should remain the same).

Several questions begged asking. If the library is changing as much as it seems to be, how can we be sure that the procedures, practices, and philosophies established twenty to thirty years ago are right for the evolving environment? Is it possible to look at these issues in an objective way–or are our views irrevocably shaped by a certain point in our professional careers? How can newer librarians compensate for a lack of institutional memory? Can we determine whether (or to what degree) institutional memory is even relevant after the institution has morphed into a very different creature?

In my opinion, this difference in perspective presents some very real challenges for me and other younger (or newer) librarians who see new opportunities and challenges on the horizon.

GENERATION X IN LIBRARY LITERATURE

I have found few articles published in library literature written from this perspective. Having gone through almost a decade of constant press coverage and "studies" of a generation of young people, I'm left to imagine how the entire library profession made it through with so little discussion of the topic. To be fair, I have caught a few listserv posts here and there with mention of the topic. And for years there have been statistical studies of libraries students' attitudes, demographics, and "aspiration surveys"[5] which, though probably quite valuable for a certain type of analysis, don't really apply to the discussion.

More recently, a few articles have been published in library literature regarding reference services for a "new generation" of library users. Among these is Manley's 1995 article, "Slackers in the Stacks."[6] Manley enumerates a litany of complaints that the "slackers" are responsible for the devolution of the English language, have contributed nothing but absurd fashion styles, and are basically irresponsible. "Slackers in the Stacks," then, is mainly a continuation of the popular trend to spotlight younger adults as an anomalous group, the likes of which the world has never seen. If the article was meant to be tongue-in-cheek, maybe I just missed it.

Catherine A. Lee, in her article "The Changing Face of the College Student," recognizes that "Xers" have been "virtually ignored in the education and library science literature,"[7] and continues to present a more in-depth and balanced exploration of the topic. She quotes freely from Strauss and Howe's *Generations*, repeating that this new generation is often defined as individuals born between 1961-1981. Lee reviews more complaints about this generation that have been spelled out in numerous articles before she presents some suggestions as to how to appeal to students of this age group.

It's interesting that these articles are written from the perspectives of librarians having to deal with a new group of younger patrons. I've had to wonder if anyone's noticed that their newer colleagues coming along might be in this same age group–whether they identify with the term "Generation X" or not.

ACADEMIC LIBRARY DEMOGRAPHICS

In my opinion, the most significant literature published on the topic at hand doesn't even mention "Generation X," though there is ample references to the "Baby Boomers." In his report, *The Age Demographics of Academic Librarians: A Profession Apart*,[8] Stanley J. Wilder documents through charts and graphs that academic librarianship is aging more rapidly than other professions, and that academic librarians under the age of 35 are a rare find, compromising only 10% of the total ARL profession as of 1994.[9] (I don't know the figures for public libraries.) The reasons for this underrepresentation are spelled out as well. According to Wilder, the age of students acquiring MLS degrees has steadily risen. In 1994, 50% of them were over 35 years of age.[10] The rate of new ARL hires has slowed as well, leaving less opportunity for recent MLS graduates. These factors, along with others Wilder explores, perhaps explains why there has been little exploration of Generation X in library literature–there simply aren't that many of us around, especially in academic libraries.

This is a concern for Wilder. He states:

> The age profile of librarianship has important implications for the health and continued viability of the profession . . . Librarianship has a record of successful adaptation, most notably in its adoption of new technologies. The next adaptation will require that librarianship translate its print-centered expertise in the evaluation, selection, organization, and preservation of information to the new digital environment. Competition for this new role will be intense, however, and the advantage will go to groups that can combine traditional 'librarian' skills with technical and managerial ones.

If one takes Wilder's admonition seriously, academic libraries need to examine what is happening to younger colleagues when they land their first job in a college or university setting. Are they encouraged and supported in their efforts to explore new ground–electronic or not? Wilder continues, "If librarianship is successful in claiming this role, the new skill mix may well be recognized in the form of expanded opportunity and higher salaries, making librarianship a career of first choice for more young people."[11]

THE FUTURE

What are the implications of this brief discussion of libraries and Generation X? I think there are several that stand out. The number of librarians who will retire in the next ten years will leave a large gap of knowledge and experience–especially regarding the details and quirks of library holdings and history. I think the traditional ideas and attitudes of librarians will probably undergo some changes as well. If I examine my like-aged peers, with whom I graduated from library school, few of them are what I would consider "traditional librarians." They range from holding academic librarian positions in relatively "normal" settings, to managing electronic resources in a manner which has creates new responsibilities and opportunities, while at the same time, separates them in outlook from other colleagues. Others seem permanently caught in temporary positions, and contemplate leaving the profession altogether in hopes of finding better salaries. I don't see any of them vocally idealistic about the profession and operating from a sense of "mission."

At the same time, the profession strikes me, at times, as bogged-down with convention (based on "tradition") that allows for little creativity in dealing with these problems. I have found it necessary to ask myself which of these "rules" are based on worthwhile professional ethics, and which have been established only out of personal preferences or institutional habit. It's not always clear, nor easy to question established practices in this environment where everyone, for one reason or another, feels threatened by the changing times.

CONCLUSION

How will librarians, who hold very traditional models of libraries, respond to colleagues who want to expand and explore and stretch the boundaries of what librarians do? These challenges will continue to grow, I feel, as technology infiltrates more traditional information-al services. At the same time, how will the best and more valuable ethics and guidelines of the library profession be communicated and illustrated to new professionals in a way that is not condescending or somehow dictated in a cookie-cutter fashion? How can librarians expect to shape their future if they are not willing to meet it head-on and accept its challenges by learning and shaping information technology?

Generation X is, of course, dead you know. In fact, Douglas Coupland, declared it dead in 1995 when he wrote, "Kurt Cobain's in heaven, 'Slacker's' at Blockbuster and the media refers to anybody aged 13 to 39 as Xers." Continuing, he wrote "Which is only further proof that marketers and journalists never understood that X is a term that defines not a chronological age but a way of looking at the world."[12] In that light, maybe a Generation X outlook has less to do with age, although I think age can play a role, but with an attitude that is experimental, open to challenge and examination–flexible to the changing environment. Above all, I think it's a perspective that looks toward the future rather than back to the past.

NOTES

1. Strauss, William and Neil Howe. *13th Gen: Abort, Retry, Ignore, Fail?* New York: Vintage Books, 1993, page 7.

2. Strauss, William and Neil Howe. *Generations: the History of America's Future, 1584 to 2069.* New York: Morrow, 1991.

3. Coupland, Douglas. *Generation X: Tales for an Accelerated Culture.* New York: St. Martin's Press, 1991.

4. Coupland refers to this phenomenon as "Legislated Nostalgia" which "forces a body of people to have memories they do not actually posses."

5. Moen, William E. "Library and Information Science Student Attitudes, Demographics and Aspirations Survey: who we are and why we are here." *Librarians for the New Millennium.* American Library Association. Office for Library Personnel Resources, 1988.

6. Manley, Will. "Slackers in the Stacks; New Generation of Young Library Patrons." *American Libraries* v. 26 (September '95) p. 856.

7. Lee, Catherine A. "The Changing Face of the College Student: The Impact of Generation X on Reference and Instruction Services." *The Changing Face of Reference.* Edited by Lynne M. Stuart and Dena Holiman Hutto. Foundations in Library and Information Science Series, v. 37. Greenwich, CT: JAI, 1996.

    8. Wilder, Stanley J. *The Age of Demographics of Academic Librarians: A Profession Apart: A Report Based on Data from the ARL Annual Salary Survey.* Association of Research Libraries, Washington D.C., 1995.
    9. Ibid., page 12, Figure 7.
    10. Ibid., page 34, Figure 18.
    11. Ibid., pages 58-60.
    12. Sign of the Times. *The Washington Times.* May 24, 1995. Part C, page 13.

History of a Library Unit and the Evolution of Its Culture from the Eyes of Two Participants: Holland Reference Services from the "Merger" (1977) to the "New Organization" (1997)

Mary Gilles
Christy Zlatos

SUMMARY. The authors explore the roots of Holland Library Public Services in two original divisional libraries, the Humanities Library and the Social Sciences Library, and chronicles its evolution through the "merger" (1978-82), the Kemp years (1983-89), the New Library planning and construction phase (1989-94), and a modern phase (1995-present). The modern phase includes a discussion of the influences of a library reorganization. Specific aspects of Holland Library Public Services culture are detailed and discussed; conclusions are drawn. *[Article copies available for a fee from The Haworth Document Delivery Service: 1-800-342-9678. E-mail address: getinfo@haworthpressinc.com]*

Mary Gilles is Head, Humanities/Social Sciences Public Services, Holland/New Library, Room 120E, Pullman, WA 99164-5610 (E-mail: gilles@wsu.edu). Christy Zlatos is Head, Media Materials Services, Holland/New Library, Room 1-C, Pullman, WA 99964-5610 (E-mail: zlatos@mail.wsu.edu).

[Haworth co-indexing entry note]: "History of a Library Unit and the Evolution of Its Culture from the Eyes of Two Participants: Holland Reference Services from the 'Merger' (1977) to the 'New Organization' (1997)." Gilles, Mary and Christy Zlatos. Co-published simultaneously in *The Reference Librarian* (The Haworth Press, Inc.) No. 64, 1999, pp. 31-43; and: *Coming of Age in Reference Services: A Case History of the Washington State University Libraries* (ed: Christy Zlatos) The Haworth Press, Inc., 1999, pp. 31-43. Single or multiple copies of this article are available for a fee from The Haworth Document Delivery Service [1-800-342-9678, 9:00 a.m. - 5:00 p.m. (EST). E-mail address: getinfo@haworthpressinc.com].

INTRODUCTION

What is presently known as Holland Library Public Services or Holland Reference Services and resides in the Holland/New Library complex results from the merger of two separate divisional libraries, the Humanities Library and the Social Sciences Library. Both of these divisional libraries were located in the old Ernest O. Holland Library and date from the time that the Holland library building was finished in 1951. This article explores the roots of Holland Library Public Services in the two divisional libraries and chronicles its evolution through the merger (1978-82), the Kemp years (1983-89), the New Library planning and construction phase (1989-94), and a modern phase (1994-present). The modern phase includes the influence of the reorganization of the Washington State University Libraries. At the end of the article, specific aspects of Holland Library Public Services culture are detailed and discussed; conclusions are drawn.

OUR DIVISIONAL LIBRARY ROOTS

The Ernest O. Holland Library, named for a previous college president, was one of the first large "modular" buildings completed after World War II. Made popular by nationally known library architect, Angus Snead McDonald, this "modular" plan was characterized by efficient low ceilings, regularized interiors, and the easy removal of interior walls that allowed flexibility for later changes.[1] To alleviate some of the criticism of the building's "functionalism" (Holland Library had 9 foot ceilings), a high-relief sculpture of a student reading a book was commissioned to counterbalance what was considered the overly severe appearance of the total structure. Dubbed "Nature Boy" by the students of the era after the Nat King Cole song, the sculpture is known today as one of the more distinctive features of our campus.

Always a devotee of efficient library operations and responsive to student and faculty needs for instruction, the then-library director, G. Donald Smith's (1946-76) evolving conception of library services reflected the flexibility of this design. In 1950, he wrote:

> The new building was designed around a plan of close, flexible, and ever expanding cooperation between the Library and the instructional and research staffs, to bring the Library into active

not passive sharing in the educational enterprise. The core of this scheme is the abandonment of the traditional "reference," "periodical," and "reserve," reading rooms, and to a large extent the abandonment of separate closed "stacks," in favor of a broad (divisional not departmental) grouping of materials of all kinds–reference, periodical, book, pamphlet, and other–in rooms so arranged as to encourage and facilitate direct student use of the resources of learning.[2]

Three divisional libraries were created for Holland Library–Humanities, Social Sciences, and Physical and Natural Sciences–and these would be assisted by a fourth division, the Readers' Services Division.[3] The staffs of the three main divisions would develop the collections and services for the division in the best way for those disciplines they served. Reference services, collection development, circulation, serial record keeping, and cataloging would occur separately in each divisional library. Government documents cataloging occurred in Social Sciences. A Technical Services Division still existed but was to be scaled down.

The card catalog was moved from Bryan Hall to the new building and later copied. One card catalog remained intact in the Readers' Services section and one catalog was separated, both author-title and subject, and appropriate parts were given to each of the three divisional libraries.

The divisional libraries evolved separately before 1977 when the Physical and Natural Sciences Library moved to a new building, the Owen Sciences and Engineering Library. Although quite a lot is known about the creation and function of the divisional libraries, very little is remembered about the re-centralizing technical functions into Technical Services Division (TSD) from the divisional libraries. For example, Social Sciences cataloging was transferred to TSD in June 1959, but government documents cataloging was later re-assigned to the Social Sciences Library and continued there into 1978.

THE MERGER

When the senior author interviewed for her position as a Social Sciences Reference Librarian and Documents Cataloger in 1971, to get help a person had to walk up to the second floor of Holland because TSD had sprawled on the first floor. The Social Sciences Library, then, with its strong walk-in trade, functioned as a de facto undergraduate library. Populated with some outrageous, outspoken people, the faculty and staff of the Social Sciences Library exhibited excellent customer relations. Someone was always available to talk with students and faculty and offer help.

On the other hand, the Humanities Library was located in an "ivory tower" on the fourth floor. Students and faculty really had to want assistance to climb the whole way to the fourth floor (the public elevator that exists today dates to the late 70s). In demeanor, the Humanities library faculty seemed reserved; they took exotic summer vacations in faraway places. They were definitely a different kettle of fish.

The two different disciplines, the Humanities and the Social Sciences, as well as the personalities of faculty and staff of the divisions were reflected in the arrangement of the divisional libraries. The Social Sciences Library had a small reference collection that had a nice arrangement by subject, i.e., history, political science, sociology, etc. Dictionaries, encyclopedias and handbooks would be paired with indexes and abstracts to make a full-service A&I section on a subject. The Humanities Library, on the other hand, was arranged by LC classification and was huge and glutted with lots of "Z" bibliographies to navigate. The Humanities Library's inclusive approach to reference collection development was very different from the streamlined approach adopted by the Social Sciences librarians.

Because Social Sciences librarians didn't do reference in Humanities and vice versa, merging the two services was a significant challenge and included classic issues that two merging companies might deal with. Questions about:

- The Reference Collection: How big should the reference collection be and how should it be organized?
- Reference Desk Scheduling: How long should the reference desk shifts be? Should there be a master schedule for the whole semester or should there be unique schedules month by month? Can we roam around the library, or should we stay put at the reference desk?
- Policies and Procedures: Can we take annual leave during the academic school year? Who's responsible for rescheduling our

shift(s) when we're ill? Can we get personal telephone calls at the Reference Desk? How long should our breaks be?

- Reference Card Catalogs: Whose style should be used? How shall we standardize?

Although the actual merger occurred in 1978, a year after the Sciences moved to the now-completed Owen Sciences and Engineering Library, much planning for the merger occurred before director G. Donald Smith retired in 1976 and Allene Schnaitter (1976-84) came on board.

The book collections were merged in LC format, TSD moved to the fourth floor freeing up the first floor, and the new, combined Humanities/Social Sciences Reference (Hum/Soc) moved to the first floor. The Hum/Soc Serial Records staffs and Kardexes merged; the circulation staffs merged and so did interlibrary loan functions. Holland Library Public Services was to include serial record, circulation, interlibrary loans, microforms, current journals, the collections (and their development) and reference services. During Spring 1978 librarians from the new Holland Library Public Services embarked on a training mission to acclimate everybody to the new subject disciplines.

In order to bring fresh new ideas to Washington State University, outside expertise was desired. A new Assistant Director for Public Services, Ronald Force, was brought on board from Ohio State University on January 2, 1979. Although Force, as Assistant Director, was supposed to coordinate public services throughout the Washington State University Libraries, the independent-minded Owen Sciences and Engineering Library resisted coordination. Although Force's job title was Assistant Director, he actually administered just the Holland Public Services. A system-wide coordination of public services was never realized.

Force did not stay long at WSU. When he left in 1982[4] the Hum/Soc librarians met together to choose a successor to be Head, Holland Public Services. Audrey Dibble, a Humanities librarian who had spearheaded much of the merger, was chosen. In addition to choosing a leader, the Hum/Soc librarians developed a list of demands. Neither Dibble nor the list was accepted by the Director.

To fill the vacancy until a new Head could be hired, two other Hum/Soc librarians stepped forward to fill in a year as Interim Head while the search got underway. Some of the members of the blossoming Hum/Soc faculty questioned whether a better tactical move than using colleagues to fill-in could have been found. They thought the group could have stuck together and told the Director no.

KEMP YEARS (1983-89)

Barbara Kemp became Head, Holland Library Public Services on June 1, 1983. Kemp came into a more honest, scaled down situation than Force experienced. She would not have to try to plan for public services on a Libraries-wide scale, nor would she have to implement the merger of Hum/Soc. The times were comparably tranquil but, also, they were becoming exciting.

New Library Director Maureen Pastine from San Jose State University, arrived in 1985. Pastine had a national reputation in our profession and soon started promoting the national participation and publication that were to have a long-term significance on our library faculty and services. Untenured librarians began creating "tenure plans" to chart their development and tenured librarians began thinking about promotion.

Innovations in technology and in user education also were making the workplace interesting. Recognizing the use of technology to solve library problems early on and the role that libraries could play in creating systems, G. Donald Smith had created the Libraries' Systems department in 1966. Early collaboration between the Libraries and the Computing Center allowed for the mixing of ideas and the sharpening of expertise. Grants were sought. The first Acquisitions system, LOLA (Library On-Line Acquisitions Sub-System), through the help of an NSF grant, came up in 1968. In 1972, Washington State University Libraries joined forces with the Washington State Library to parlay the Libraries' expertise into augmenting the acquisitions system, with its capacity for fiscal reports, into a component of the emerging statewide bibliographic system. This system would become the Washington Library Network (WLN) that was organized in 1977.

Washington State University Libraries then used WLN as its bibliographic utility. The Libraries' own online catalog was developed in-house with WLN software; an early command system was brought up in the early '80s.[5] The catalog was named "Cougalog" (after the WSU cougar mascot) in a contest that was held during National Library Week in 1986. A user-friendly interface to the Cougalog, called EZSEARCH, was introduced in 1988. With financial support from a major corporation, Software AG, plans were made to utilize technology developed at WSU (specifically a serials control module) along with modules from other universities to make an integrated system that would be marketed under the name Tapestry.

In Holland Public Services, Barbara Kemp went to the ALA Midwinter Conference in 1987, and came back with the idea for the first Holland CD-ROM product, *Compact Disclosure*. Compact Disclosure ran on a 286 PC that initially sat on a utility cart that was wheeled into the "Reference Work Area" (RWA) every night upon closing for safekeeping. Little did we anticipate the explosion of technology that is happening today.

In response to increased interest in user education, especially in Holland Public Services, a system-wide Head of User Education was hired into the Libraries in 1988. A systematic approach to user education was also a keen interest of Pastine's. This position that reported to the Director of Libraries was charged with developing a program that would aid librarian-educators as well as develop an approach to traditional courses with library components such as English 101.

THE NEW LIBRARY PLANNING AND CONSTRUCTION PHASE (1989–1994)

In 1989, the planning and design phase for the construction of a Holland library addition began in the Libraries. Because the original E.O. Holland Library had long been out of space, the news of funding for the addition was received as a welcome breath of fresh air. Although planning started almost immediately, our euphoria was short-lived because the Libraries again lost administrators.

Pastine left the Libraries as Director in 1989 and Barbara Kemp followed her exodus from the Libraries shortly thereafter. As Interim Director, long-time professor and friend-of-the-Libraries, Donald Bushaw served for a time until he became ill and Donna McCool, the WSU Libraries' Associate Director, took over. As Interim Head, Holland Public Services, senior author Mary Gilles served for nearly three years until 1992.

Our present Library Director, Nancy L. Baker, came to us from the University of Washington in April, 1991. Upon arrival, she encountered so many vacancies that she decided to stagger filling the positions in order to stabilize the organization. Among the vacancies was the Head, Holland Public Services. Another was the Assistant Director for Library Systems position; the incumbent resigned to spearhead the Tapestry project.

The New Library Addition Project was then in full swing, and Allan W. Bosch, who had experience with a large building project, the Kenyon College Library, was hired as Head, in July, 1992. Like Force before him, Bosch also offered useful outside expertise as the former Associate Director of the Kenyon College Library. Like Force, Bosch also encountered challenges in carrying out his official duties. Notably picking up the Library Addition Project in midstream, Bosch admirably ran with it until its completion. Like Force, Bosch left the Libraries early, in June, 1995, to pursue academic library building consulting from the Florida Keys.

MODERN PHASE (1994–PRESENT)

The Modern Phase began with the move into the addition in May, 1994; the addition was named the New Library. The entire Libraries' staff participated in the moving effort; t-shirts, refreshments, and prizes were given away during a move that took place at the end of Spring semester, 1994. Holland reference librarians coordinated and moved the reference collection and all the A&I literature under the direction of Mary Nofsinger, Head of Reference. Today, the New Library is one of the most modern buildings on campus.

After plans to implement the Tapestry product as our integrated online catalog (that utilized our own serials control module) did not work out, the Libraries turned its attention to the many commercially available online "turnkey" library systems on the market. The decision occurred shortly after the Libraries' switch to OCLC as a cost-saving measure from WLN near the beginning of 1994. After some consideration, and with the blessing of the new Assistant Director for Library Systems, John Webb, the Libraries purchased an Innovative Interfaces system as a joint catalog along with Eastern Washington University. The WSU/EWU catalog is called "Griffin" in honor of the mythical creature that is half Cougar-like (WSU mascot) and half Eagle-like (EWU mascot). The text-based version of Griffin came up in 1995 followed by a Web version in 1997.

A year-long planning process, initiated by Director Nancy Baker and culminating in May 1997, produced Values, Mission and Vision statements for the Libraries, along with an updated organization. The Head, Holland Public Services position was left vacant after Allan Bosch's departure, along with several others, to provide flexibility in adapting the organizational structure.

In the spring of 1997, the Hum/Soc librarians discussed options for the local organization. Some of the "givens" resulting from the planning process included: (1) a scaled-down Hum/Soc with former units (the Brain Education Library and the Architecture Library) reassigned; (2) the "loss" of a librarian position to implement the new organizational structure; and, (3) a step down in the reporting line from the Director to an Assistant Director for Public and Research Services, a newly created position. Concluding that the Head's duties did not warrant a full-time position, Hum/Soc librarians recommended an elected, three-year, term position to be called "Chair" and filled from among the tenured librarians in the department. Director Baker agreed to the concept, but not the title, and Hum/Soc embarked on an experiment in self-management.

An election last summer resulted in the senior author's initiating the redefined Head position. The incumbent retains most of her former duties and the role is more one of a facilitator than an administrator. Department decisions are made by the group. While not calling themselves a "team" the Hum/Soc librarians have adopted several aspects of that approach to work. The group is also committed to the recently adopted Library Values, which include "trust, openness, integrity and respect."

HOLLAND PUBLIC SERVICES CULTURE TRAITS

From the chronology of our roots in the two divisional libraries until the present, the following points distinguish our Holland Public Services Culture:

OUR LOVE/HATE RELATIONSHIP WITH OUTSIDE AUTHORITY/EXPERTISE: Our history shows that over the years we have desired outside authority or expertise especially in our administrative position to show us the way but we do not always appreciate the authority when he or she arrives.

OUR INDEPENDENT STREAK: We regard the Administration as useful for securing resources and facilities; just avoid telling us what to do.

OUR UNIQUE AND DISTINCTIVE CULTURE APART FROM THE REST OF THE LIBRARIES: Although the "merger" occurred twenty years ago, most of us still regard ourselves as either Hum or Soc. Because Holland reference librarians are hired for their collection development expertise as either Hum or Soc (our collection development budgets never merged), this view has been reinforced over time.

We are the only public services unit within the Libraries without a definite space with walls. This dates from the time of the "merger," when the Sciences moved to a new, complete building down the hill and Holland stayed in the original E.O. Holland Library building. At present, Holland Public Services shares the Holland/New Library complex with other units including Manuscripts, Archives and Special Collections (MASC), Media Materials Services (MMS), the Library Administrative Office (LAO), and the Technical Services Division (TSD). Although it may sound corny, walls make a difference.

Because we "compete" for collection development dollars and are most often compared with the Owen Sciences and Engineering Library, we regard them as "the other." They are definitely better activists and they can readily rally their faculties for support. As the Holland Reference Services has been "saddled" with a huge undergraduate population, we embrace everybody. This tendency combined with the absence of a distinct space/territory has made Holland Reference Services less partisan.

OUR LOYALTY/FAIRNESS TO OUR FELLOW HUM/SOC COLLEAGUES: Although we have differences, we basically like each other. There are no long-standing feuds between individuals. We don't have a "class system" with newer librarians assigned all of the undesirable reference shifts.

OUR SUPPORT FOR NEW PROFESSIONALS AS LIBRARY FACULTY COLLEAGUES: Although the senior author wonders whether the support offered new professionals today even approaches the nurturing she received from colleagues in the Social Sciences Library in the '70s, the Holland Reference Services environment offers young professionals many opportunities for advancement and growth. Collection development responsibilities, user education, teaching credit courses, electronic resources management, and the new various applications for technology, including distance education, make the environment interesting.

COMING OF AGE?

Humanities/Social Sciences Public Services is in the first year of the experiment in self-management. Is this approach a better match for the culture? It's still too soon to know, but the authors offer some initial impressions.

In our history we have noted the early departures of individuals hired to be our administrator. In response to this trend, we then pinpointed two aspects of our culture that define us: "our love/hate relationship with outside authority/expertise" and "our independent streak." In consideration of these two aspects, the redefined Head, Holland Public Services position (that is elected to a three-year term and keeps all former departmental responsibilities) seems very sensible as long as (1) the incumbent can keep the duties of both roles balanced (facilitator/administrator and reference librarian/user educator/departmental liaison); (2) the facilitator/administrator workload remains relatively stable; and, (3) there's agreement of all involved (the incumbent and the Hum/Soc librarians) that this approach meets the department's needs and works satisfactorily. So far, both Holland Public Services and the Hum/Soc librarians seem to function well under the new regime of part-time administration. Time will tell whether the Hum/ Soc librarians ever again have the need for a full-time administrator.

In our culture we have also noted "our unique and distinctive culture apart from the rest of the Libraries." Although this is still very much a part of us, an aspect that defines and comforts us, perhaps this also may be changing a little bit, especially in our younger librarians. Hum/Soc librarians have always participated on Libraries-wide committees and task forces but these days our young librarians seem to form better collaborations (with collaborators from both Holland and Owen) and they enjoy them more. Maybe it's the emerging technology that sparks the collaboration in creating a library skills course over the Web, designing Web applications for the Libraries' Web-based online public catalog, Griffin, working with the many databases and CD-ROM products the Libraries' own, or designing the Libraries' Home Pages.

CONCLUSION

In writing this history and defining our culture, we are reminded of how organizational decisions linger for years. We are also reminded of how long it takes for an implemented decision to catch on here at Washington State University Libraries. From the era when G. Donald Smith was Director, we inherited both a divisional library concept and the early adoption of technology. This early adoption and our long experience with in-house database design are apparent today in our library staffs' facility with technology and our easy implementation of our new library catalog. From the era when Maureen Pastine was Director, we inherited national participation and publication for tenure that were to have long-term significance. We also inherited the Libraries' Head, User Education position, designed to coordinate this function Libraries-wide. Although the first Head, User Education was hired in 1988, the actual coordination aspect of that position is just beginning to happen.

Our history and culture define us; we believe that our recent history more readily takes into account our roots than ever before. Our 1996 Planning Committee for our new organizational structure was comprised of both library faculty and staff from throughout the Libraries' units with myriad considerations. Our new organizational structure makes the Holland Public Services' experiment in self-management with its redefined Head, Holland Public Services position possible.

Just what effect our recent decisions–our Holland/New Library, our switch to OCLC, our new Innovative Interfaces catalog, Griffin, or lastly, and most importantly, our new organizational structure–will have on us far into the future remains to be seen.

NOTES

1. For a discussion of "functional" library buildings, see Macdonald, Angus Snead, "New Possibilities in Library Planning," *Library Journal* 70:2 (December 15, 1945); 1169-74. For a discussion of the Holland Library Building Project, see Maloney, John W, "Modular Library Under Construction: The State College of Washington, Pullman, Washington," *Architectural Record* CIV (July 1948); 102-9.

2. G.D. Smith, "Projected Development of the Ernest Holland Library of the State College of Washington." Unpublished paper, dated May 25, 1950 (University Archives, Office of the President, 1948-60); 2.

3. For a discussion of Smith's divisional library notions, see Smith, G. Donald, "The Divisional Organization of the Readers Services at Washington State College,"

in *Changing Patterns of Reference Service.* Seattle, WA: University of Washington, Bureau of Governmental Research and Services, 1953; 11-19. For a discussion of the divisional library scheme over time, see Smith, G. Donald, "Library Organizational Structure," Unpublished memorandum to Pauline Lilje, dated June 14, 1976. (Siegfried A. Vogt Collection, reprinted in *The Reference Librarian.*

4. Presently, Ronald Force is Dean, Library Services, University of Idaho.

5. Information about WSU library automation, WLN, and the Software AG, Tapestry Project comes courtesy of Terry Buckles, Information Technology, Washington State University, Pullman, WA 99164-3075.

Jim and Alison Do User Education:
English 101 and Beyond
at Washington State University Libraries

James Elmborg
Alison Manning

SUMMARY. The authors use English 101, their primary program, as a springboard for a discussion of teaching as a library function. Both view the one-hour presentation that is commonly done in libraries as grossly inadequate; they offer solutions that are working at Washington State University Libraries. These include cultivating better relations with departments in order to increase the time spent for library instruction, understanding different pedagogy styles and departmental cultures, creating Web modules to reach more students, and focusing attention specifically on one clientele, i.e., freshmen. *[Article copies available for a fee from The Haworth Document Delivery Service: 1-800-342-9678. E-mail address: getinfo@haworthpressinc.com]*

The User Education office in the Washington State Libraries faces issues common to many academic libraries. Our primary problem seems to result from our growing pains. In the past, we have done a basic one-hour presentation for the English 101 program (freshman composition). This presentation has been repeated for other classes

---

James Elmborg is Head, User Education, Holland/New Library, Room 102, Pullman, WA 99164-5610 (E-mail: elmborg@wsu.edu). Alison Manning is Reference Librarian, Holland/New Library, Room 120C, Pullman, WA 99164-5610 (E-mail: awalker@mail.wsu.edu).

[Haworth co-indexing entry note]: "Jim and Alison Do User Education: English 101 and Beyond at Washington State University Libraries." Elmborg, James and Alison Manning. Co-published simultaneously in *The Reference Librarian* (The Haworth Press, Inc.) No. 64, 1999, pp. 45-52; and: *Coming of Age in Reference Services: A Case History of the Washington State University Libraries* (ed: Christy Zlatos) The Haworth Press, Inc., 1999, pp. 45-52. Single or multiple copies of this article are available for a fee from The Haworth Document Delivery Service [1-800-342-9678, 9:00 a.m. - 5:00 p.m. (EST). E-mail address: getinfo@haworthpressinc.com].

(Intensive American Language Center, upper-division English, and others) with various changes to suit the sophistication level of the students. It has become increasingly obvious to us that the one-hour presentation is inadequate. Our building is complex, our databases proliferate at an alarming rate, search engines become more sophisticated, our catalog undergoes periodical transformations, and still, our freshmen come in with the same basic skills as ten years ago. We believe it is imperative to do more to teach these students, since there is significantly more to teach. Yet still we struggle against the constraints of our allotted hour.

English 101 is our primary program, and during the past year, there were one-hundred and twenty-five sections of this freshman composition class, with each section enrolled to about twenty-four students. Our program reached approximately 3,000 students during the 1996-97 school year. Two librarians–Alison Manning and Jim Elmborg (the authors of this article), taught the overwhelming majority of these classes. Reference librarians also share responsibility for teaching classes. Each librarian has responsibility for three classes per semester. Eleven librarians contribute to this cause, thereby covering sixty-six of the one-hundred and twenty-five. The remaining sixty or so classes are taught by Alison and Jim. During this past year we have seen an increase in the number of classes requested because many English instructors have asked for more than the minimum instruction. We attribute these requests to two causes. First, these instructors recognize as we do that the one-hour introduction to the library is insufficient. In addition, we have spent the year cultivating a collaborative working relationship with the freshman English program. As a result, many instructors now see us as major contributors to their classes, and they request second, and in some cases, third visits to the library for formal instructional sessions.

During the past year, we have worked to build a strong relationship with the English Department. We believe we have the respect of the English faculty because we provide consistently strong instruction and because we have experience teaching these courses. In preparation for this article, we discussed our English 101 program and why it works. We both decided that, on paper, it can't work. The organization, scheduling, and teaching of these classes is impossible given the resources we have. In reality, however, the program works, and it works quite well. Since English 101 is our primary instructional program, we decided to use it as a springboard for a discussion of our discussion of teaching as a library function. We feel we have a successful program, but we would be the first to acknowledge we have problems. We aim to provide an honest discussion of the successes and problems in our program, and in the process discuss some of the issues facing library instructors today.

WORKING WITH OUR ENGLISH DEPARTMENT COLLEAGUES

Our top priority for this academic year was to improve relations with the English department. Besides teaching the English 101 classes, our public relations efforts have included attending introductory orientations for instructors, participating on their electronic discussion lists, and even teaching some library classes in the English department's computer lab. We try to convey to them–in all these ways–that we value their input and will work with their needs. Jim has been the primary liaison to the English department, a job made easier by his previous training and experience as an English instructor. While they might seem familiar on the surface, English departments and libraries have very different cultures. Our success with the English department is a delicate balancing act which is successful only to the extent that we can work in both the library and English department worlds.

We are called on to represent the libraries formally twice a year. At the beginning of each semester, we go to the orientation meeting for English 101 instructors. At these meetings, we are called upon to discuss new developments in our instructional program. We try to avoid conspicuously representing the libraries at these meetings. Instead, we attempt to engage the instructors in a discussion about research and our mutually compatible roles in the research process. The major challenge is to convince these instructors of the value of research. This challenge is made more difficult by specific conflicts within the English department. Often, young instructors who have not developed a teaching pedagogy approach writing instruction by encouraging their students to discover their identity through writing. These instructors suggest that writers learn to write by exploring their inner voices–giving a voice to the thoughts and feelings inside. Writing, as seen by these instructors, is the process of drawing out a "self." Teachers who teach this way tend to devalue research and put emphasis on the mental or emotional processes of the student. More experienced instructors understand that a good composition class involves explorations outward. College writing is a social process, and writers need to see themselves fitting into a world of other writers. That world of other writers exists, of course, in the library. We approach the English 101 program by becoming partners with the writing program administrators as they attempt to develop a sound pedagogy among their often-inexperienced Teaching Assistants.

Such a strategy can be risky, however, since we are, by definition, "outsiders" to the English Department. Jim has tried to develop an open style of communication with the administrators of the writing program, who tend to support the role of research in the writing classroom. Their support helps us to advocate an approach that fits in to the writing curriculum. An openness to innovation also helps us to be seen as an asset to the English department. Rather than insisting on a single format of the instructional session, we try to tailor our teaching to the assignment of the given class. We find that our classes go more smoothly when there is a specific assignment due at the end of the class. We ask the instructors to design the instructional session into their research assignment. We suggest that students should have a five-item bibliography by the time their session is finished. For this suggestion to have any weight, the instructor needs to make the assignment a requirement of the class. Doing the bibliography forces students to use all the skills we hope to impart in the session. We try to approach the rest of the session with as much flexibility as possible. We work with the instructors to make the session valuable for their individual needs.

While the English department appreciates our flexibility, we have had problems defining how flexible to be. Often, English instructors request content we find inappropriate. They will ask that their English 101 students be introduced to much more sophisticated tools and strategies than they are equipped to handle. They sometimes bring us assignments we know will create problems at the reference desk either because the resources are limited or the students will be incapable of working with the databases. This kind of situation causes our librarians a great deal of stress because we want to be seen as supportive and constructive, and we tend to be insecure about our standing in the academic community. We have learned this year that when we make suggestions to English instructors, they are usually grateful and adjust their assignments immediately. Our resources change rapidly, and often instructors have not taken the time to think through assignments. The entire process goes better when we assume professional control over our subject and our classes. The instructors feel better about the direction of the class and so do we.

WEB MODULES

As we have suggested, over the past year we have become increasingly aware that the one-hour instructional session is not adequate for conveying all that our freshmen need in order to use the library. If we focus on high-level thinking skills, students get lost in the stacks. In addition, the material we want to convey has become more complex, and one hour is not enough to really "teach," the important concepts. We are in the process of developing several strategies for dealing with these problems. We have been aggressive about recruiting further involvement in the writing program. English 201, 301, and 402 (all advanced writing courses) are the fastest growing component of our program. We enthusiastically recruit these courses and work to keep them once they have come for a session.

Within the Freshman Composition classes, however, there has not been room for expansion. English instructors have been hesitant to devote more class time to library instruction, with some fearing a loss of control and direction. For these instructors, we have developed a sequence of Web-based instructional modules. These modules were developed by a team of librarians who worked closely with a team of English instructors. From the beginning, we have been aware that two things have to happen for on-line instruction to succeed. First of all, the modules have to be professionally presented. Our students are sophisticated consumers of media, and we felt that to be successful, the modules had to be polished in both look and intellectual content. Secondly, no matter how good these modules were, they would not work without acceptance among the English 101 instructors. We felt that teamwork between librarians and English instructors would accomplish both these goals, as well as give us another place to increase our presence in the English department.

We began the development process with a fall meeting attended by all the representatives of the English department and the libraries. We agreed that for the process to really work, we would need to develop concepts and foundations from which to proceed. We also found that we needed to confront issues of institutional culture. The English department functions quite differently than the libraries. Instructors are fairly autonomous in their affairs, and they tend to philosophize more than librarians. These differences led to some impatience among the librarians, who wanted to get on with the business of developing the modules. We soon realized that we need these brainstorming sessions, however, because the issues raised by the English instructors were precisely the reason we needed them. They understood the needs of the instructors and the goals of the course in ways we did not.

The modules developed over the course of the entire year. We spent the first three months meeting once every two weeks. This was "brainstorming" time. We planned the form of the modules, their organization and architecture. We tried to confront the problems of pedagogy on the Web. This activity culminated with a formal class in HTML conducted by the university technology guru. Over the winter break, we all took a three day intensive class on writing for the web. The class included both skills and concepts, in other words, "how to" and "how to do well." This class marked the beginning of our writing phase. During the spring semester, we divided into four teams, with one librarian and one English instructor per team. Each team was responsible for a module. The modules included: *Introduction to the Library, Introduction to Griffin* (our online system), *Searching for Periodical Articles,* and *Advanced Search Strategies.* Near the end of the spring semester, we met again and did a workshop on the modules. We agreed at this point to leave the "ego" portion of our project behind and treat the modules as community property. We tried to see what worked and what didn't with an eye toward revising the entire set of modules toward a common goal. We had discussions about the importance of graphics, the effective use of hypertext links, how much control to allow students, and general aesthetics. At that point, we went back to the modules and began to revise.

It would be nice to say that this process was tidy and clear, but that would not be true. There were several tense moments when librarians and English instructors aggravated each other, and people began to feel quite possessive of their work and took criticism personally. Fortunately, we all saw a bigger purpose and worked through the problems. One English instructor in particular emerged as the leader of their group. She facilitated participation and conveyed concerns for the English instructors. In order to put the modules in place for the fall semester, this instructor will work during the summer in the User Education office developing support materials for the Web modules. She will be responsible for implementing the program in the fall, and helping us to evaluate the success of the program. The modules are available for viewing at http://www.wsulibs.wsu.edu/usered/AML/home.html

WORKING WITH FRESHMEN

Often, our colleagues question our commitment to undergraduate education. At its most extreme, there is a belief that library instruction is ineffective and that first-year students are not intellectually ready to deal with something as sophisticated as an academic library. We disagree, of course, and suggest that education is a long process, and that freshmen will one day be juniors and seniors. We must acknowledge, however, that teaching freshmen is sometimes aggravating. They lack maturity and commitment, and they often react inappropriately to formal education. Still, we find teaching freshmen more rewarding in many ways than teaching more advanced courses.

In order to help the growth of the User Education program, Alison decided to concentrate much of her time and effort on the freshman composition program. Alison's participation in the User Education program also allowed Jim to substantially decrease his teaching load, and have more time to concentrate on the administrative details of the User Education program. Even though Alison does teach other classes than English 101, she still prefers working with freshmen. In fact, an overwhelming majority of the classes she teaches are English 101. Such a choice probably requires explanation.

She believes that even though freshmen can be difficult to work with at times, teaching them can be an extremely rewarding experience. Because Alison teaches so many English 101 classes, she has a good grasp of the learning level of the students. They may be confused by the large quantity of resources in the library, or they may not understand the layout of the library. Just the sheer size of the library intimidates freshman. Alison's goal is to try to relieve some of that intimidation. She strives to maintain a friendly environment in the English 101 session, and she makes an effort to give students ways of reaching her for additional help. Usually that additional help will occur at the reference desk, and their relief is very apparent when a familiar face is there to greet them. Alison has found it challenging to present basic library skills in an increasingly complex library environment. Basic library skills just don't seem enough anymore. Reality dictates, however, that we accomplish all we can within a one-hour class. Alison believes that if she can prepare students to ask questions about the process of finding articles instead the very general (and dreaded) "How do I find an article?," half of the battle has been won. And maybe, just maybe, they will then be able to transfer what they learned into other classes they may have throughout their time at WSU.

Often English 101 is the only chance for formal instruction that the libraries have with students. Some students will be more exposed to the library than others through their course work at WSU. However, we find it appalling that students might leave WSU without ever entering the library's doors. Ideally, we would like to structure our program so students return for library instruction year after year. Unfortunately, we have been unable to incorporate this coherence into the curriculum, and presently we lack the resources to teach that many classes. Covering all the English 101 sections has been challenging enough. We accept that we will not see all students a second time in a formal library instruction session, and we have focused our efforts on the English 101 program.

CONCLUSION

While we are fairly satisfied with our instructional program at the present time, we face the same chronic frustrations as most academic libraries engaged in instruction. We continue to struggle to define ourselves both in the library and in the academic community at large. Within the library, we are often seen as tangential to "real" librarianship. In the academic community, we still lack an appropriate venue for our work. In an era of rapidly expanding tools and resources, we feel more and more limited by the constraints of the one-hour orientation. Still, we find ourselves teaching in exciting times. Technological advances make our instruction central to the research process, and we find our faculty turning to us to help their students understand the rapidly changing information landscape. The challenges we face make this an important time to be in library instruction.

Lessons of a Decade:
An Instructional Experiment Matures

Paula Elliot
Alice Spitzer

SUMMARY. In 1987, a new two-semester freshmen-level course in World Civilizations was piloted at Washington State University. Included within the course was a library component offering the question analysis that seemed appropriate to a richly historical, interdisciplinary course. The authors involved with the course from the very beginning, discuss their decade of work on the World Civ project in terms of the project's successes and unrealized hopes, its collegial component, and its growth and adaptation over the years (including examples of library assignments). As a university-wide project, World Civilizations was a forerunner of other projects nationwide and an outstanding example of librarians collaborating with teaching faculty to promote instruction. *[Article copies available for a fee from The Haworth Document Delivery Service: 1-800-342-9678. E-mail address: getinfo@haworthpressinc.com]*

BACKGROUND

In 1987, after several years of university-wide meetings on general education reform at WSU, and a year of intensive curriculum develop-

Paula Elliot is Head, Humanities Collection Development, Holland/New Library, Room 120K, Pullman, WA 99164-5610 (E-mail: elliotp@wsu. edu). Alice Spitzer is Reference Librarian and Professor of General Education, Holland/New Library, Room 120G, Pullman, WA 99164-5610 (E-mail: baars lag@wsu.edu).

[Haworth co-indexing entry note]: "Lessons of a Decade: An Instructional Experiment Matures." Elliot, Paula and Alice Spitzer. Co-published simultaneously in *The Reference Librarian* (The Haworth Press, Inc.) No. 64, 1999, pp. 53-66; and: *Coming of Age in Reference Services: A Case History of the Washington State University Libraries* (ed: Christy Zlatos) The Haworth Press, Inc., 1999, pp. 53-66. Single or multiple copies of this article are available for a fee from The Haworth Document Delivery Service [1-800-342-9678, 9:00 a.m. - 5:00 p.m. (EST). E-mail address: getinfo@haworthpressinc.com].

ment activity, a new two-semester freshman level course in World Civilizations was piloted. Librarians were involved in the process from the beginning.[i] The course had been conceived as not only an introduction to various cultures of the world but also as an introduction to academic life, recognizing the academic community as a subculture in its own right with which students needed to become familiar and comfortable. In this context, as librarians, we wanted to join with faculty to take the mystery out of academic research. At the time, although the literature had long been advocating that librarians participate in curriculum development, it was difficult to identify practical literature which described the kind of large-scale core curriculum planning in which we found ourselves included. Now, as the curriculum reform movement flourishes nationwide, articles describing involvements similar to ours frequently appear. Time, someone said, is a great equalizer.

Since the 1970s, librarians at WSU had been involved in teaching library use thorough the required English 101 course, which underwent revision to dovetail with the World Civilizations course.[ii] In English 101, the topics students wrote on were of a contemporary nature; librarians emphasized how to locate journal articles in the traditional manner, and relied upon a standard worksheet distributed to all sections. As a two-semester course, World Civ, as it was called, suggested a new approach. With two semesters of exposure, librarians speculated that they could offer a cumulative learning experience introducing the question analysis which seemed so appropriate to a richly historical, interdisciplinary course content.

To differ formally from library instruction in English 101, librarians and faculty in World Civ decided to emphasize the identification and use of specialized encyclopedias–a largely unknown and vastly underutilized resource–and techniques for locating and evaluating books. Faculty developed original assignments for their respective sections, guided by stated objectives[iii] and informed by librarians' suggestions. Inspired by the famous Earlham College model and then-current writings on critical thinking in library instruction, we created a package of exercises and experiences which were successful when used in the self-selected pilot sections of the course.

Ten years ago, when we wrote about the development of the World Civ course, we were optimistic about our work with the pilot sections and looked forward to fully implementing our ideas. But all did not go as planned. How has this project changed since those heady, idealistic early days of the course in its pilot phase? And what impact have the changes had on our reference librarians? This article reviews our successes and our unrealized hopes in the World Civ Library Project.

CHANGE AND COMPROMISE

Once World Civ was out of its pilot phase, and serving 3,500 students each semester, faculty idealism became inevitably tempered with disgruntlement. "Too much to cover!" was the refrain, familiar to any librarian struggling for a toehold in a class. The World Civ Group made several adjustments in the course "covenant," a formal agreement made by the many faculty teaching the many sections of the course.[iv] Teaching faculty formulated unanticipated definitions of "content" and "extras," placing the library component and a required report of a cultural event in the latter category.

A compromise was reached: A library project would be required in the first semester (GenEd 110) and optional in the second (GenEd 111); a cultural event would be required in the second semester and optional in the first. Such wrangling preceded the compromise, we thought that most of the faculty teaching GenEd 111 would drop the library assignment, but this has not been the case. That over half the second-semester World Civ faculty have chosen to include the required library experience attests to the value they place on the library's role in their classes and in the education of newly entering freshmen.

Numerous logistical obstacles have prevented us from implementing sophisticated concept-based library education in this class: Although two semesters of World Civ (GenEd 110-111) are required for graduation, it is impossible to ensure that a student will take the course in its intended chronological sequence, or in conjunction with English 101, or even in the freshman year. Detailed, considered assignments have given way in many cases to standardized, fill-in-the-blanks exercises which prove a student's ability to identify various resources but not necessarily to research a paper. In the early days librarians usually met with classes to introduce the assignment and potential approaches, but as the numbers grew larger, the librarians' efforts were diverted instead to helping the faculty member create a workable assignment with carefully written out instructions and steps. Since virtually all English 101 classes come to the library for instruction, many World

Civ students perceived the librarian's visit to their World Civ class as repetitive of their English 101 experience, and tuned out even though different skills and tools were being addressed.

SETBACKS AND SURPRISES

Although we anticipated and addressed the clustering of many sections' assignments due at the same time, and headed off similarity of assignments among sections, many students were vying for limited resources. The vagaries of automated scheduling, faculty advising and student decision-making quickly discouraged our hope for sequential instruction over two semesters. Despite our collaboration with teaching faculty, each semester there were assignments which assumed resources the library didn't have and/or skills and background in library use that the students didn't possess, failing to recognize an increasing diversity in students' backgrounds.

During the first semesters of full implementation in 1993 and 1994, the reference desk suffered shock beyond any recollection. It seemed as though despite all our efforts to prepare teaching faculty, classes and reference librarians, each time a World Civ student approached the reference desk, a full reference transaction was often required. Most nightmarish of all was the hostility among our own reference faculty over whether these hordes should even use the library for the course. It was clear that we needed to develop some kind of standardized help: student handouts, more rigorous faculty consultation, and some education for librarians.

THE FACTOR OF COLLEGIALITY

The ability to solve some of these problems was rooted in the good will between those teaching World Civ and their long-time librarian colleagues. During the annual summer workshop for World Civ faculty, the librarians talk about new developments at the library since ours, like most, is in a constant stage of change. At this time we also discuss particularly successful World Civ library assignments, and post a sign-up sheet so that assignment due dates are spread relatively evenly throughout the semester.[v] The liaison librarians make themselves available to work individually with faculty–particularly those teaching the course for the first time–in the development or modification of assignments, offering a set of faculty guidelines.[vi] Teaching World Civ demands notoriously rigorous preparation, so new faculty often are very appreciative of a librarian's assistance. Several experienced faculty continue to consult with librarians each year. Without exception, all members of the World Civ faculty, perhaps thirty in a given semester, send us copies of their assignments which we use to inform our reference colleagues and keep for our information at the reference desk. Over the years, communication has improved among reference faculty concerning the World Civ assignments, and though individual librarians' philosophies may differ, the population of World Civ students has been successfully assimilated into the ever-heavy traffic at the desk.

GROWTH AND ADAPTATION

One of our problems has been the overuse of successful assignments by several professors. In addition to the possibility of plagiarized papers, it creates a run on certain heavily used materials which are then mutilated or "disappear," leaving other students empty-handed and frustrated. One of the most popular is the "biography" assignment, in which students choose a historical personage to research. This assignment has the advantage that students often grow genuinely proprietary toward their subjects, but there is often scant information on some of the lesser-known figures. Since there is no line in the acquisitions budget to support General Education, and the book budget is designed to reflect the needs of academic departments, we have successfully written intra-university grants to purchase additional library materials on heavily researched topics. We have also worked with some faculty to restructure their assignments so that students don't need to check material out of the library.

Some of the problems we have seen relate to the variety of backgrounds students bring to the class. To help "level the playing field" some professors informally survey students regarding their familiarity with basic WSU library resources. (Librarians have not been invited to monitor this survey; we question the accuracy of the students' self-assessment.) Students in these classes who feel the need for extra help with the library assignment arrange to meet in the library with the teaching assistant (or sometimes the professor), who has met previously with a librarian. The faculty's lament "Too much to cover!" precluded any in-class administration of potentially valuable pre- and post-testing of students. Students only comment on their library experience when completing their course evaluations at the end of each term.

Because most of the assignments are designed to require the use of specialized encyclopedias, we developed a handout of appropriate titles, grouped into broad categories, with call number locations. Our Pink Sheet, as it has become known, has saved countless hours of librarians' time by giving the students a structured place to begin their research. A conceptual process occurs when faculty and librarians encourage them to think of a topic in terms of the broader context within which it falls (e.g., period, country or part of the world, discipline such as religion or art or politics), and the Pink Sheet assists them in an independent head start which they find satisfying. In many of the classes students are assigned a topic, or choose it from a list of unfamiliar terms, and often have no idea whether Mansa Musa is a place, person, or religious movement, let alone what part of the world or time period he/it might belong to. Although some faculty want to discourage the students' use of encyclopedias in their research, others agree with the librarians about their value. We have observed that awareness of these resources affects the students' subsequent approach to research for other classes.

GOOD, BAD, UGLY AND BACK–
EXAMPLES OF ASSIGNMENTS

What are examples of assignments that have been developed over the years? Which have worked, which haven't, and why? Observation suggests to us that those faculty who have consulted with librarians generate more successful library experiences for their students.

As mentioned, the biography paper has been one of the most frequently used assignments. The better organized of these gives students a list of names (with variant spellings), requires that work be done in stages, and limits the way(s) in which the topic should be addressed. Several examples use worksheets to guide students through finding information on their topic in the textbook, specialized encyclopedias and books.[vii] They are required to put a person in a larger context–where and when the person lived, what related terms are associated with the person, again using a worksheet. Students also respond to worksheet questions applying rudimentary principles of evaluating a source. They observe chapter titles, illustrations, acknowledgments, preface, introduction and bibliography to determine a book's potential usefulness in preparing their 600-word biographical essays.

As an example of individual faculty approaches, to get his students "in the door" one professor devised an innocuous worksheet-based hunt to locate and use things like the copy machines, Dewey Decimal and Library of Congress stacks, bound periodicals, and the on-line catalog. This exercise has a personal appeal, and has been adopted by some of the professor's colleagues. Students look for Library of Congress call numbers which match or are close to their initials; Dewey numbers which resemble their ID numbers, and complete other small tasks which acquaint them with the physical layout of the library. Students then apply this acquaintance in pursuing a biography project.

Group presentations, more often seen in the second semester classes, require an annotated bibliography with a variety of types of sources including periodical articles. The broad themes that groups are assigned–such as the fall of Soviet communism, legacy of imperialism, role of women, racism, nuclear balance of power, environmental issues–are tied to specific current events such as the ethnic conflict in Bosnia, civil war in Rwanda, and destruction of the Amazon rain forests.

Although books, encyclopedias and, sometimes, journal articles are the norm, one professor asked students to also locate a film, video, photograph, song, poem, painting or sculpture related to their topic. At first this flustered both the students and librarians but once we got into the spirit of it (and understood better the professor's flexibility), it became an enjoyable task for all concerned, especially because it drew on librarians' untapped knowledge in areas seldom addressed during regular reference transactions. Another project, in a linked "skills" class, has students creating multimedia modules on their topics.

Faculty have found interesting ways to structure a student's written product. One has had them write obituaries, in standard obituary form. The trick is that students can only use things that would have been known about the person at the time of his/her death. Much of the literature about Muhammed, for instance, discusses his impact on later centuries, so students had to be careful to weed out such information.

This same professor, another semester, asked students to write travel guides to a particular city at a particular time in its history, again being careful to write only what could be verified for that historical period.

Another assignment asks students to select a time and place before 1500, choose a character (real or imaginary) and write a diary of one day in the life of this character. The object was to create or recreate the person's life as realistically as possible taking into account such aspects as food, housing, family relationships, work, illness, recreation, religion, arts and crafts. Once students got over the panic of feeling they had to find information on all of these, they got into the research and wrote quite creatively.

Another professor has collected postcards showing pre-1500 objects and places. Students select a postcard, purely on the appeal of its image, and then use the subject of the image as a basis for learning how to find and use specialized encyclopedias and books. The end result is a contextual and bibliographic worksheet, and a 1-2 page process paper detailing their experiences in the library. The element of choice on the students' part has made this assignment fairly successful.

Although librarians work with most of the twenty to thirty faculty teaching in any given semester, problem assignments do emerge. Sometimes students, when told to "pick any topic from the index to the book", are so lost they don't know where to begin. Librarians often spend time talking students through the process of choosing a topic before they even begin to work on their library project.

Students sometimes take the professor's instructions too literally-"pick a part of the world, tell where it is and what language was spoken, what foods were eaten, what clothing was worn, etc., in 1500." They are frustrated when they can't find a book that says, specifically, "In the year 1500 Incas ate guinea pigs." It was impossible to convince them that the professor meant something more general, perhaps a culture's agricultural or hunting practices in relation to food supply. Librarians met with the professor to suggest some possible in-class remarks.

Also, there have been cases where a well-intentioned professor asked students to locate and summarize a certain number of references used in the textbook's bibliography. Unfortunately the library didn't own some of them at all (and they were out of print so we could not have gotten them easily even if we had known about the assignment in time), and those that we did own disappeared almost immediately after the first few students hit the library.

While our on-line catalog is under development, students experience problems related to the catalog's instability. Materials missing from the shelves may be unaccounted for in the catalog. Inexperienced students may not find material because they're not looking under the right word and aren't prepared to try alternatives. Those new to the system don't know if they've done something wrong or if it's "the system."

CONCLUSION

Despite occasional faculty and reference staff complaints, and the expected few undergraduates posturing at the desk, student evaluations show that the students appreciate their library experience in this more often than not. Our observations are borne out in the recent *Report on Student Evaluations of the World Civilizations Core:* "A large majority, 65%, of students strongly or moderately agreed the library research project increased their research skills." We would like to be able to assess in more detail *what* skills they believe increased, and which transfer into library activities for subsequent courses.

Library requirements for many classes demand the use of the World Wide Web or complex information databases. For library-shy beginners, our current blend of print-based, on-site experiences serves its purpose. Over a decade, we have resolved many troublesome issues, and traditional though it may be, we now enjoy an established, manageable program.

Reviewing the last ten years, it is tempting to conclude that our involvement with the World Civilizations library instruction effort yielded little that remains extraordinary today, though it may have been in its time. It is gratifying to observe the growing involvement of librarians in similar programs around the country.[viii] The recent literature validates many of the principles which we acted upon ten years ago, and continues to advocate commitment to strong faculty-librarian contact, librarian presence on university curriculum committees, clear statements of goals and agreed-upon course objectives, staggering of sections' assignments, and to the extent that budgets allow, adjustment of library priorities to respond to course demands.

From the podium at ACRL in 1989, we emphasized that our relationship with teaching faculty was the single most crucial element in making this instructional effort work. This subject remains fresh in recent literature, which regularly continues to urge communication between teaching faculty and librarians: "It is vital that librarians . . . work with other campus units and participate in campuswide programs . . ."[ix] The consistent appearance of this admonition suggests that such relationships may not yet be the norm.

Our own professional development has taken us in directions unimagined a decade ago. Other librarians have become involved in large campus projects such as the General Education Committee, the Honors Program, and Extended University Services.

Director of General Education Richard Law believes that the connection between the General Education program and the library has potential for expansion into higher-level courses in the undergraduate curriculum. "The involvement of librarians in General Education reform on this campus was insightful from the beginning. A stated outcome of core curriculum courses is the student's ability to retrieve information. As we teach students to become lifelong learners, I am more convinced than ever of the importance of library skills. In positioning ourselves to offer a layered sequence of library instruction, we are just beginning to collaborate."[x]

NOTES

i. Elliot, Paula & Spitzer, Alice. The Collegial Connection: Working with Teaching Faculty to Create a New Course." *Proceedings of the Fifth National Conference of the Association of College and Research Libraries.* Chicago: ACRL/ALA. 1989, 144-146.

ii. Spitzer, Alice. "Bringing an Interdisciplinary World View to English 101–The Library's Involvement." *The Reference Librarian*, vol. 29, New York: The Haworth Press, Inc., 1989, 113-122.

iii. Appendix 1.

iv. Available from the Office of General Education, Washington State University, Pullman, WA 99164-2634.

v. This system has been adopted at the University of the Pacific, whose program reported by Fenske and Clark takes an approach similar to ours (Rachel F. Fenske and Susan E. Clark. "Incorporating Library Instruction in a General Education Program for College Freshmen." *Reference Services Review*, Fall 1995, 69-73).

vi. Appendix 2.

vii. At the request of English instructors, library instruction no longer utilizes worksheets in English 101, in which automated periodical indexes are introduced with hands-on instruction. Over the years, the approach to library instruction in

English 101 has evolved quite separately from that in World Civ rejecting early models which linked the experiences in the two classes.

viii. Some programs are surveyed by Hannelore B. Rader, in "Information Literacy and the Undergraduate Curriculum." *Library Trends* 44:2(Fall 1995), 270-278.

ix. Maurie Caitlin Kelly. "Student Retention and Academic Libraries." *C&RL News*, December 1995, 757-759.

x. Law, Richard G. Interview with the authors, June 1997.

SOURCES CONSULTED

Elliot, Paula and Spitzer, Alice. "The Collegial Connection: Working with Teaching Faculty to Create a New Course," *Proceedings of the Fifth National Conference of the Association of College and Research Libraries.* Chicago: ACRL/ALA, 1989, 144-146.

Fenske, Rachel F. and Susan E. Clark. "Incorporating Library Instruction in a General Education Program for College Freshmen." *Reference Services Review*, Fall 1995, 69-73.

Kelly, Maurie Caitlin. "Student Retention and Academic Libraries." *C&RL News*, December 1995, 757-759.

Law, Richard G. Interview with the authors, June 1997.

Rader, Hannelore B., in "Information Literacy and the Undergraduate Curriculum." *Library Trends* 44:2 (Fall 1995), 270-278.

Spitzer, Alice, "Bringing an Interdisciplinary World View to English 101–The Library's Involvement." *The Reference Librarian*, vol. 29, New York: The Haworth Press, Inc., 1989, 113-122.

APPENDIX 1
Librarians' Objectives for Students
in World Civilizations Classes

Concept-Based Objectives. A student completing a library project should be able to:

1. Apply contextual clues in articulating project goals and information needs.
2. [Optional] Distinguish "scholarly" from "popular" monographs and periodicals.
3. Recognize the merits and drawbacks of general and specialized encyclopedias.
4. Apply rudimentary selection criteria in choosing reference sources, books and articles.
5. Defend choices of sources.

Skill-Based Objectives. By executing a library project in World Civilizations 1 and 2 (GenEd 110-111), a student should become familiar with:

1. The use of "Griffin," the libraries' on-line catalog, for the retrieval of books using call numbers. The card catalog is of secondary importance.
2. The use of dictionaries and encyclopedias, for general information and suggestions for further reading.
3. [Optional] The use of basic published indexes to periodical information (Reader's Guide, Social Science and Humanities Indexes, The New York Times Index) and/or their electronic counterparts.
4. The components of a bibliographic citation.
5. The role of reference librarians and other library personnel; regulations and protocols for the use of WSU Libraries.

APPENDIX 2
Librarians' Tips for Faculty
Teaching World Civilizations

Preparation

- Become familiar with the library's concept-based and skill-based goals for the World Civ library project, as stated in the accompanying document, "Educational Objectives in Library Use for Students in World Civilizations Classes."
- Consult files of established projects for ideas and for standardized worksheets.
- Keep your project simple and relatively brief. It is intended to acquaint students with square-one principles of scholarly investigation.
- Let the World Civ librarian know your plans. The librarians will alert reference faculty to your students' particular needs. The librarian will also try to ensure that there are adequate library materials for your students' use. She can also offer suggestions toward a more effective assignment.
- Identify a due date, or, more ideally, a series of due dates for your assignment in consultation with the World Civ librarian. *To best serve the students and maintain the availability of library materials, it is essential to stagger World Civ library project due dates throughout the semester.* The librarian will keep a master calendar.
- Give a copy of your printed assignment in all its parts to the librarian and to the general education office.
- Familiarize your TA with the project and its intended goals. It's important that the TA approach this project with an understanding of *freshman* needs and experience rather than graduate-student needs. Encourage your TA to meet with the World Civ librarian to discuss your section's project.
- Create a list of topics from which students can choose and sign up. Allow the World Civ librarian to check for availability of materials in advance of sign-up.

Preliminary Assignments

- Be aware that beginning students are generally leery about approaching the library. Their initial responses can range from curious to downright intimidated.

APPENDIX 2 (continued

- Create or choose an existing orientation assignment which engages students in acquiring some of the stated skills.
- Distribute up-to-date library handouts and instruction sheets. Procedures, locations, and current sources change frequently at the library. Don't risk using last year's help sheets; find out what's new.
- Take some class time to explain the assignment. Use class time, too, to explain rudimentary procedures for finding and evaluating information. Consider having students write anonymously questions and concerns about the project; react to them in a later class period.
- Plan a due date close to the time that the handouts are distributed. If the class syllabus indicates a final due date of the last day of school, your students will be in the library on the next-to-last day of school trying to remember what they're supposed to do.
- Assign retrieval tasks which make intellectual use of materials found. If you ask students to identify books or journal articles, ask them also to react to information found in those sources.
- Remind students that the library project will be completed in a series of steps; it cannot be accomplished in one crash visit to the library.
- Encourage students to make effective use of reference librarians by having thoughts organized and questions in mind.

Final Product

- State clearly your expectations for the writing component of the library project.
- Emphasize that this project should include some rewriting and revision.
- Emphasize the importance of evaluating information, and taking responsibility for information chosen.
- Consider using bibliography forms rather than requiring a formal bibliography. Students may not yet have been introduced to bibliographic protocols; the form encourages awareness of the components of a citation.
- Entertain in-class written or verbal questions along the way. Build frequent progress checks into the project.
- Suggest that students with writing problems seek help at the writing lab.

The Klaipeda University Library in Lithuania: An Essay by the Washington State University Libraries' Library Fellow

Janina Pupeliene

SUMMARY. The author, Library Director at the University of Klaipeda (Lithuania) and Washington State University Libraries' Library Fellow, writes about her own library in the context of other Lithuanian academic libraries and emerging consortia in Lithuania and the European Community. Both the Consortium of Lithuanian Libraries' project, the Lithuanian Integrated Library Information System (LIBIS), and the European Community's project, the Trans-European Cooperative Scheme for Higher Education (TEMPUS), are specifically noted. The author also offers both her impressions of American academ   ic libraries gathered during her experience as a Library Fellow based at Washington State University Libraries and her hopes for the future of academic libraries in Lithuania. *[Article copies available for a fee from The Haworth Document Delivery Service: 1-800-342-9678. E-mail address: getinfo@haworthpressinc.com]*

The Library Fellows Program, funded by the United States Information Agency (USIA) and administered by the American Library

Janina Pupeliene is Library Director, Klaipeda University Library, Donelaicio a. Klaipeda 5800, Lithuania (E-mail: j.pupeliene@libr.ku.lt).

[Haworth co-indexing entry note]: "The Klaipeda University Library in Lithuania: An Essay by the Washington State University Libraries' Library Fellow." Pupeliene, Janina. Co-published simultaneously in *The Reference Librarian* (The Haworth Press, Inc.) No. 64, 1999, pp. 67-73; and: *Coming of Age in Reference Services: A Case History of the Washington State University Libraries* (ed: Christy Zlatos) The Haworth Press, Inc., 1999, pp. 67-73. Single or multiple copies of this article are available for a fee from The Haworth Document Delivery Service [1-800-342-9678, 9:00 a.m. - 5:00 p.m. (EST). E-mail address: getinfo@haworthpressinc.com].

Association, I am sure, is well known among American librarians. The program was established in 1987 and, in 1993, it was expanded to include non-U.S. librarians to enhance their professional experience and allow them to obtain expertise in certain areas.

In 1996, 17 librarians came to the United States and I am proud to be the first Lithuanian librarian invited to participate in this program.

BIOGRAPHY

After graduating from the Vilnius University (Lithuania) in 1976, I have worked in academic libraries in Klaipeda (Lithuania). Much of this time was spent working in small pedagogical libraries and college libraries specializing in preschool teacher education. My experience covers many library activities including acquisition, cataloguing, circulation, and reference. Since 1991, I have been the library director at Klaipeda University.

ABOUT KLAIPEDA (CITY)

Klaipeda, the only port city in Lithuania on the coast of the Baltic Sea, was founded in the 13th Century. In the present day, Klaipeda is not only a port but also a major cultural centre of Western Lithuania. It has a population of more than 200,000. There are three large libraries there: a regional public library (the Ieva Simonaityte Library), a municipal public library, and the university library.

KLAIPEDA UNIVERSITY AND LIBRARY

Klaipeda University was established in 1991 and it is the youngest among 15 universities and higher education institutions in Lithuania. Our University is modeled after higher education systems in Western countries, including the United States. At present, there are 3,952 students in main, master's, and doctoral studies. The training of specialists at our university strongly favours the industry, transport, trade fleet, and fishery enterprises of a port city. Other specialties, such as ethnology, history, philology, evangelical theology, geography, ecology, and recreation, cover the history and culture of Western Lithuania as well as the region around Klaipeda.

The Klaipeda University Library was established as a separate department with the opening of the university in 1991. There is a central library and five branch libraries. Different from many American universities, Klaipeda University has no campus. Its faculties with their branch libraries are spread in a long area along our coastline, which is not convenient for users from other faculties or for organizing our library work.

Total library stock at the Klaipeda University Library is more than 460,000 copies of 150,000 titles. There are many more copies than titles because our academic libraries are still responsible for providing students with textbooks. That takes a big part of our library's money and time.

Annually, our library acquires 15,000 new copies of more than 6,000 titles. About 70% of them are assigned to the branch libraries of the University faculties; the rest remain in the central library. Purchased books comprise only 40% of our annual acquisitions and come from our vendor, the National Library Collector, as well as from other bookstores and publishers. We receive the greatest number of books from abroad, which are sent to the University Library as gifts. Lithuanian émigrés, various foreign organizations and societies donate these publications.

All collection development, including the purchasing of books and the subscribing to serials, is concentrated in our library's Acquisitions department. This practice is standard for most Lithuanian libraries. At Washington State University Libraries and in other libraries I visited in the United States, collection development is split among groups of reference librarians who have direct contact with library users. This contact with the public, in my opinion, is a big plus.

As with most other Lithuanian libraries, our central library building and branches were not specially built to be libraries. That is the main reason why our library collection is closed for the reader's access. This kind of service uses more library personnel and takes much of their time which could be better utilized providing reference services for users.

Our circulation activity in Central and in our branch libraries is based on two divisions: a lending department where users can borrow books to use at home and a reading room. The reading room is the most popular because students always can find a copy of their textbooks and current journals there. It functions similar to a reserve room in an American academic library.

For many reasons our library, like other Lithuanian libraries, is not service-oriented. Besides the earlier mentioned library space and closed stacks problems, Reference and User Education are not yet important components in Lithuanian libraries.

We have no specially designated reference areas in our branch libraries. The reference collections that exist, because of poor library budgets in most of the branches, are very small. We are trying to concentrate the most valuable and general publications in our Central library, where we have a small Reference department.

As we have no OPAC yet, our readers have to look for requested literature in the card catalogues. The union card catalog, which reflects our library collection since 1991 and includes all of our branches, is located in the Central Reference Department. Information about book locations is available by phone.

Visiting here, talking with American colleagues, and "walking" in the Internet, I realize how important Reference and User Education will be in the digital library age. The evaluation of electronic sources and teaching critical thinking skills to users will make service a leading role of libraries.

MODERNIZATION OF LITHUANIAN ACADEMIC LIBRARIES THROUGH EFFORT AND NEW CONSORTIAL ARRANGEMENTS

As a young and developing library, naturally Klaipeda University Library's structure is still being formed and the size of the book stock as well as the books' locations continue to change. The University itself is still being organized. During the last five years, some new faculties emerged, research centers opened, and many new disciplines were established in the curriculum.

In the middle of these changes and constant domestic problems, the Klaipeda University Library, along with other Lithuanian academic libraries, is active in library automation processes. These processes are going very slowly and, in most cases, progress comes with great effort from libraries, themselves without much support from either the government or the university administrations.

Since 1990, when Lithuania restored its independence, tremendous political, social and economic reforms have been implemented. That is why the state is not yet able to finance libraries, as well as other cultural and educational institutions, in a proper way. Some librarians are leaving their jobs, libraries can not afford to buy new books, implement new technology, build or reconstruct their buildings. However, there is some progress in the development of national librarianship and modernization of libraries.

In 1994, the Consortium of Lithuanian Research Libraries was established to help the automation processes in the libraries. In 1996, 16 libraries held membership in the consortium. Klaipeda University Library holds a membership in this consortium, too. The Consortium's main goal is to create the Lithuanian Integrated Library Information System (LIBIS).

As Lithuania has no such comparable institution as the OCLC in the United States, the establishment of this Consortium and the common efforts to create LIBIS give all of us hope to have a shared database in the near future. At present, every library in Lithuania is creating its bibliographic records originally.

The first step towards LIBIS is done. Four academic libraries, located in our capital, Vilnius, including the Vilnius University Library, the Vilnius Technical University Library, the Vilnius Pedagogical University Library, and the Police Academy Library, are sharing a union catalog called "BIBLIO."[1] In the near future, our library and Siauliai Pedagogical Institute Library will join this catalog.

In addition to the LIBIS project, all six Lithuanian academic libraries noted above are participating with colleagues from the Netherlands, Denmark, and Sweden in the common European Community project, TEMPUS.

The TEMPUS (Trans-European Cooperation Scheme for Higher Education) project aims is to plan, build, implement, and develop automated library systems and Internet resources for the Lithuanian libraries, to educate and support their staff. The TEMPUS project began its work in 1995 and will continue for three years.

At Klaipeda University Library, the automation process started in 1993. Only the cataloging subsystem, as a part of our integrated library information system, has been installed at the time of this writing.

Our electronic catalog has the same "UNICAT" software as Lithuanian National Library. All our bibliographic records, which numbered 18,000 in 1996, are made in UNIMARC format.

As the young university library, we presently benefit from the support received from the other academic libraries through these projects. In the future, we look forward to becoming a stronger collegial supporter and contributor.

In addition to the two consortial arrangements and their projects noted above, all 15 academic libraries in Lithuania are members of the Methodological Council of Academic Libraries. The home office of the Council is located at the Vilnius University Library.

CONCLUSION

After this short overview of the Klaipeda University Library and the situation of academic libraries in Lithuania, you can imagine how useful it has been for me, as the director of a young university library, to get acquainted with the American library system and to learn about its present situation as well as its directions for the future.

The Washington State University Libraries, my host library through the Library Fellows Program, opened a new addition in 1994 and brought up a new, on-line Innovative Interfaces library catalog "Griffin" in 1995. Both offered me a transition process I could watch; I feel that the Washington State University Libraries was the right place for me to experience these directions.

I leave the United States feeling myself very enriched with ideas for my own library's future, the warm hospitality of my American colleagues, and the beauty of Western America's nature.

I am ready to make more progressive changes at home.

NOTE

1. This catalog is the only Lithuanian online catalog available through the Internet at <http://www.vu.lt/university/library.html>.

Guest Editor's Note: By the time this article is published, more important changes in Lithuanian libraries will have occurred. Klaipeda University is participating in each of the three following projects: (1) Concerning the LIBIS project, the union catalog of Lithuanian research libraries is starting and available at <http://lnb.lrs.lt/

index.html>; additional information may be found at <http://www.ktu.lt/local_en/ fram5.htm>. (2) Concerning the TEMPUS-PHARE project, a joint catalog of six Lithuanian higher schools libraries is available at <http://www.opac.vu.lt/>. (3) A Project LABT (Lithuanian Academic Library Network) has just started; information is available on the Kaunas Technology University home page, <http://www.ktu.lt/ local_en/fram5.htm>.

Holland Library's
Electronic Resource Librarians:
A Profile of These Positions

Elizabeth Caulfield Felt

SUMMARY. Holland Library, the Humanities and Social Sciences Library at Washington State University, currently utilizes the services of four reference librarians who work as electronic resource librarians. This article examines why the electronic resource librarian positions were created, how they have developed and changed over time, and what the future may hold for them. *[Article copies available for a fee from The Haworth Document Delivery Service: 1-800-342-9678. E-mail address: getinfo@ haworthpressinc.com]*

INTRODUCTION

In May 1994, a new addition to Washington State University's Holland Library was opened. Along with the new building came new furniture, bookshelves, and a lot of new computer equipment. The then Head of Holland Public Services (Allan Bosch) decided at that time to adapt two reference positions to carry additional responsibilities for the maintenance and upkeep of the reference CD-ROM products, as well as other computer-related duties. In addition, these two

Elizabeth Caulfield Felt is Social Science Reference and Electronic Resource Librarian, Holland/New Library, Room 120I, Pullman, WA 99164-5610 (E-mail: felt@wsu.edu).

[Haworth co-indexing entry note]: "Holland Library's Electronic Resource Librarians: A Profile of These Positions." Felt, Elizabeth Caulfield. Co-published simultaneously in *The Reference Librarian* (The Haworth Press, Inc.) No. 64, 1999, pp. 75-112; and: *Coming of Age in Reference Services: A Case History of the Washington State University Libraries* (ed: Christy Zlatos) The Haworth Press, Inc., 1999, pp. 75-112. Single or multiple copies of this article are available for a fee from The Haworth Document Delivery Service [1-800-342-9678, 9:00 a.m. - 5:00 p.m. (EST). E-mail address: getinfo@haworthpressinc.com].

positions would act as central liaisons between Holland Reference and the Libraries' Systems Office.

The two individuals chosen (B. Jane Scales and Lou Vyhnanek) already had interests and skills in working with electronic resources. They were the people others always turned to for help with problems related to these new technologies. The position title changes made official what was already happening in the work performed by these individuals. In keeping with the traditional collection development boundaries in Holland Reference Services, one librarian became the "Electronic Resources Librarian, Humanities" (Scales), and the other became the "Electronic Resources Librarian, Social Sciences" (Vyhnanek).

A third electronic resources librarian position was added a year later, in 1995, when a Holland reference librarian vacancy occurred. The "electronic resource" concept was added to this position with the expectation that this position could help the other electronic resource librarians with CD-ROM maintenance, troubleshooting, teaching classes in the use of technology, and other computer-related activities. The job was advertised nationally and titled, "Social Science Reference and Electronic Resources Librarian." In addition to experience in reference and social sciences collection development, the position required "professional experience with a wide range of electronic information resources such as CD-ROM in a network environment, the Internet, and Gopher; facility with microcomputers; basic knowledge of computer networks" and preferred "demonstrated ability to teach colleagues and staff about electronic resources."[1] This position was filled in July 1995 by the author (Elizabeth Caulfield Felt).

In addition, there is a fourth position that isn't titled electronic resource librarian but still carries responsibilities for the support of these resources and should be included here. As originally created, the position was titled Government Publications/Datafiles Librarian. Charged with "overseeing the United States and Washington State depository programs . . . serving as the WSU liaison to the Inter-University Consortium for Political and Social Research; [and] providing specialized reference service relating to the use of documents and the ICPSR datafiles,"[2] in addition to participating in the general reference service at the Holland reference desk, this newly-created position was filled in the Fall of 1996 (by Hyon-Sook Suh).[3] Because nearly all ICPSR materials are now in electronic formats, and because government documents are being published more and more in electronic formats, and because this librarian has taken on the management of the library's Geographic Information Systems (GIS) collection, this position will be included here as an electronic resource librarian.

THE JOBS EVOLVE

After the creation of the first two positions, "Electronic Resource Librarian, Humanities" and "Electronic Resource Librarian, Social Sciences," it soon became apparent that this was an unrealistic method of dividing the duties attached to these positions. Many of the electronic resources available in the humanities and the social sciences are similar. For example, they are produced by common vendors (Silver Platter, WilsonDisc, NISC, DynaText, etc.) and share similar search engines and set up procedures.

The significant differences among the electronic resources available at Holland Library are between government document and non-government document products. The federal government began producing data on CD-ROM in the mid-1980s, and most of the early CD-ROMs came with sparse documentation and unfriendly user interfaces.[4] Although the situation has improved somewhat, there is still no standard in government document CD-ROM production. Interfaces and software are wildly different and documentation is still not good. Keeping up-to-date on all of the government documents discs and making them available to the public is a difficult and time-consuming job. Managing government document CD-ROM discs became so overwhelming that the duties were split in 1996 between the Electronic Resource Librarian, Social Sciences, and the new Government Publications/ Data Files Librarian.[5]

In summary, despite the original subject-specific position titles, the social science librarian became the government documents-electronic resource librarian and the humanities librarian became the non-government documents-electronic resource librarian. Position descriptions were eventually changed to reflect these changing responsibilities (see Appendix 1, Position Descriptions).

The third electronic resource librarian acts as back-up for CD-ROM maintenance and coordination. This happens only rarely when others are on vacation or out-of-town and then there is often very little to do. This position is consulted from time to time by the others, when advice is needed (e.g., where a new product or machine should be located, which of several products should be networked or not, etc.). The electronic functions performed in this position are troubleshooting and working with the Libraries Home Pages, which is discussed at length later.

JOB DESCRIPTIONS

Appendix 1 is a compilation of past and present job descriptions of the four individuals working as electronic resource librarians. An examination of these job descriptions shows both the presence and the coexistence of electronic resource responsibilities alongside the more traditional collection development and reference service duties of the Holland librarian. They also show the increasing amount of time devoted to electronic resources.

In the first job description (Lou Vyhnanek's), the 1993 title "Coordinator of Humanities/Social Sciences CD-ROM Databases" was replaced by "Electronic Resource Librarian, Social Sciences," reflecting the initial splitting of CD-ROM responsibilities and the renaming of the position. However, even with fewer responsibilities, the amount this position's time spent on electronic resources has grown from 30% to 35%.

As shown in the second job description, the Electronic Resource Librarian, Humanities (Scales) took over non-government document CD-ROM maintenance and coordination in 1994 with an expectation that 25% of her time would be spent on this enterprise. With the addition of another electronic resource librarian, and an increase in duties in other areas (coordinating extended degree library services and teaching a library and information skills course over the Internet for extended degree students called University 300), the 1996 job description for this position shows a reduction of electronic resource activities to 15% of her time.

Looking at the third pair of job descriptions, the Social Science Reference and Electronic Resource Librarian (Felt) had a substantial increase in time spent on electronic resources, from 5% in 1995 to 15% in 1997. Much of this time represents work with the ever-expanding Libraries Home Pages, troubleshooting computer problems, and liaising with the Library's Systems Office.

From 1995 to 1996, the most recently created electronic resource librarian position had a title and responsibility change. Originally hired as the "Government Documents/Datafiles Librarian," the position quickly evolved to "Government Documents and GIS Coordinator." This evolution happened for several reasons. In 1995, ICPSR (the Inter-collegiate Consortium for Political and Social Research, the WSU Libraries main non-government supplier of datasets) switched its system of delivery of datasets from the physical delivery of reel tapes, CD-ROMs, and printed codebooks to delivery by electronic file transfer. This move greatly reduced the amount of time WSU Librarians spent ordering and managing this information. As originally designed, the Government Documents/Datafiles Librarian would have had a small role in geographic information systems. With additional time to devote to GIS, and having experience, education and interest in the area, Suh has taken on a leading role in GIS coordination within the libraries. With 25 to 30 percent of her time spent working with electronic resources, her newest job description shows that Suh's position is heavily involved with technology.

THE EVOLUTION CONTINUES

As evidenced in the job descriptions, Holland Library's electronic resource librarians are responsible for CD-ROM coordination and troubleshooting; liaising with the Systems Office; maintenance and creation of the Libraries Home Pages; selection, maintenance, and instruction in the use of government documents CD-ROMs and GIS services; and general instruction in the use of technology.

CD-ROM Coordination

According to the WSU Libraries Task Force on Access to Electronic Resources, "Acquiring electronic resources is not the same as acquiring print material."[6] In Holland Library, as in many large academic libraries, material is selected by collection development subject specialists. While this strategy works well for print materials, it can sometimes cause problems when transferred to the ordering of electronic materials. Owning this material doesn't make it readily accessible to patrons. There is an additional need for equipment, programming, etc., before they are useable resources. It is this additional need that calls for the electronic resource librarians to play a role in the purchasing decisions for CD-ROM and other electronic materials.

In September 1994, the WSU Libraries Task Force on Access to Electronic Resources issued a report that includes an appendix outlining guidelines for electronic resource selection (see Appendix 2, Task Force Report). Despite these guidelines, there have been some purchasing mishaps. The first problem occurred before the Task Force's report was released with the purchase of the *Oxford English Dictionary* on CD-ROM. Although the first release of this disc worked fine in Holland reference, the second release proved troublesome. Because of software incompatibilities, the database would not allow the user to print. It was very frustrating for patrons who used the electronic version only to discover they needed to go to the print edition to get a copy of what they had found.

A second problem occurred with the purchase of the Electronic HRAF (Human Relations Area Files). E-HRAF required that the text be copied and pasted to a word processor to be printed. For a multiplicity of reasons, Washington State University Libraries do not offer word processing programs on public terminals. E-HRAF was also a security risk as it made all computer files and drives accessible to any user. The solution that was eventually arranged utilized a computer in an empty Holland librarian's office where a user could access both E-HRAF and the necessary word processor. E-HRAF would only be available during office hours, which vary greatly from the hours the library is open. Fortunately, the E-HRAF software upgrade has fixed these problems. A word processor is no longer needed for patrons to print from E-HRAF, and this database is now available at a public workstation.

Because of these problems and the potential for more, the electronic resource librarians made a proposal to the Holland reference librarians (see Appendix 3, Untitled, Pre-Purchase Responsibilities/Post-Purchase Responsibilities). Responsibilities for purchasing electronic resources would be divided between subject specialists and the electronic resource librarians. The subject specialists would compare the content of the product with available resources. The electronic resource librarians would arrange testing the product, analyze the technical capabilities, and help locate the necessary equipment for running it. The proposal was accepted informally by the Holland reference librarians.

Many libraries are moving away from CD-ROM databases, towards full-text indexing and abstracting services, either tape-loaded at home or accessed via the Internet. At WSU Libraries, librarians are also evaluating the available options of what are becoming significant purchases. Through the aid of the electronic resource librarians, this evaluation is going a bit more smoothly. The collaboration between subject specialists and electronic resource librarians has been a successful one.

Liaison to the Systems Office

Communication between Holland reference and the Systems Office has not always gone smoothly. A recent informal departmental policy that enabled electronic resource librarians to act as intermediaries has helped. The policy dictates that Holland reference librarians in technological distress should first report any computer-related problem to an electronic resource librarian. This would enable the electronic resource librarian to fix "simple" problems and teach the reference librarians how to correct the problem in the future. More difficult problems would be forwarded to the Systems Office for help, with an indication of the level of urgency. As an electronic resource librarian would be the one contacting the Systems Office, this insures that the Systems Office would not be notified multiple times of the same problem. The electronic resource librarians would also be able to help the Systems Office prioritize the problems. This is not a written policy, and it has not been universally accepted. Some reference librarians still contact the Systems Office without using the electronic resource librarians as go-between, although it has improved with time. It is also not always clear if the Systems Office agrees with the prioritization of problems by the electronic resource librarians.

In an effort to promote communication and get high priority work done, the Systems Office proposed this idea: once a week, a Systems Office technician would be scheduled to come down to the reference area to work on specific things that need to be done, such as putting new software on a machine or adding a new CD to the Libraries' LAN. This proposal was accepted and the arrangement is working well. The regular meetings seem to have helped communication between departments, especially concerning the day-to-day, non-emergency needs.

For a while, the electronic resource librarians met bi-weekly with the staff of the Libraries Systems Office to discuss new developments, old problems, and any other issues concerning both departments.

These meetings were at first very informal. Often, not everyone showed up; often, there was no agenda. Recently, these meetings have been formalized. There is now a formal library committee and its membership has been extended Libraries-wide. The Electronic Resources Committee is comprised of the four Holland humanities and social sciences librarians, the user education librarian, two science librarians, the Assistant Director for Library Automation and the Systems Office Librarian. The Committee has regularly scheduled meetings, a chair, an agenda, and circulated minutes. The Committee plans to look at the broad question of electronic resources, our goals and our plans to reach them.

Libraries' Home Pages

The third Holland electronic resource librarian (Felt) has responsibility for coordinating the creation and maintenance of the Libraries' Home Pages. To this end, this position chairs the Libraries' WWW Subcommittee of the Database Coordination and Implementation Committee (DCIC), the Committee charged with maintaining the Libraries' Home Pages, and is a member of the University-Wide WWW Advisory Board.

Washington State University Libraries' traditional departmental library structure has evolved today into basically two camps, the "humanities and social sciences" and the "sciences." The Libraries' Home Pages and their maintenance also reflect this structure. When the Home Pages initially were created, there was a science electronic resources librarian who did day-to-day maintenance on the science pages; a Holland electronic resource librarian (Felt) worked on the humanities and social sciences pages. The two of them split everything else. When the science electronic resource librarian left WSU, the Holland librarian took over nearly all the work on the Home Pages except for the science pages, which several different librarians continued to maintain. The Systems Office maintains the server hardware and software, and a Systems Office technician also makes additions or corrections from time to time.

Recently the WWW Subcommittee decided to let Subcommittee members who were willing to maintain/create their own sites gain access to those directories on the server. For example, the user education librarian has access to the user education directory but to no others. Subcommittee members, representing library departments, have begun creating and maintaining their pages in this way.

This electronic resource librarian position has a high profile as "Webmaster" of Washington State University Libraries' Home Pages; the librarian's personal name and e-mail address are listed on many of the pages. As the central point of contact for the deluge of problems, questions, or comments concerning the Libraries' Home Pages, this librarian receives much e-mail. The Webmaster responds by fixing the problems or answering the questions herself, if possible, by delegating queries to another Subcommittee member, or by bringing them to the Subcommittee for a discussion and joint decision. So far, this process has worked well.

Washington State University Libraries, like other libraries in the country, are expanding their catalog and indexing services onto the Web. This expansion creates essentially more complicated pages and potentially involves many more people. The question about who maintains the interfaces on these new services is becoming more and more important. At the Libraries, the WWW Subcommittee is working in conjunction with other Libraries' committees as evidenced by the Subcommittee's newly approved mission statement (see Appendix 4, World Wide Web Subcommittee of DCIC). Two of the Web Subcommittee's collaborators are the OPAC Subcommittee and the Collection Development Committee.

Government Documents/GIS Coordinator

Keeping up with the information produced and disseminated by the federal government is a difficult and time-consuming job. Having one librarian coordinate the ordering, processing, maintenance, and instruction for use of these materials has become, for Holland Library, a necessity. In order to keep abreast of what is happening in electronic government information, Hyon-Sook Suh belongs to a number of listservs, primarily GOVDOC-L and MAPS-L. Suh also reads *Administrative Notes* which is the newsletter of the Federal Depository Library Program. Suh keeps her fellow reference librarians and users notified of new developments and products through e-mail announcements, the development of handouts, and one-on-one and group instructional sessions, and articles in *Library Update*, a WSU Libraries newsletter published for the WSU faculty.

In addition to managing the Libraries' federal government documents, Suh coordinates the Libraries' GIS and geospatial data applications. This involves assisting and consulting GIS data inquiry for the WSU Libraries. She has created a listserv, WSUGIS-L, to provide WSU GIS users with information about the services available at the library. Suh also maintains the GIS data set collection and provides special reference service for GIS users in Holland Library. This involves assisting in the extraction of geo-referenced census data sets and providing basic instruction on the use of GIS software: ArcView, Wessex ProFiler, etc. Suh is the back-up librarian for those needing to order ICPSR datasets. With fellow librarian Siegfried Vogt (Head, Social Sciences Collection Development), she is involved in overseeing the collection of ICPSR data sets.

In the coordination of Government Documents and GIS services, this electronic resource librarian works with the selection and ordering of materials, as well as with the creation of handouts and the teaching of users. This position requires a thorough knowledge of the material, as well as the ability to teach librarians and students what is available and how to access it.

Instruction in the Use of Technology

User education is an additional responsibility that falls upon the Holland electronic resource librarians. For the last four years, the Libraries have offered free Internet classes to university students, employees, and the community at large. These classes have covered a wide variety of topics: Internet Basics, FTP, Gopher, Listservs and E-Mail, the World Wide Web, Web Search Engines, HTML, and more. Organized by the Libraries' User Education department, electronic resource librarians are expected to volunteer as teachers.

The Libraries have also offered computer classes for library employees. These have covered such topics as: Using Windows, Using E-Mail, Microsoft Word, Microsoft Access, Microsoft Excel, and more. Organized by the Libraries' Systems Office, electronic resource librarians again volunteer to teach sessions.

In addition to the formal classes mentioned above, electronic resource librarians are also involved in more informal instruction. Once a month, a part of a weekly Holland reference meeting is devoted to the demonstration of a new electronic resource. As often as not, an electronic resource librarian will demonstrate a new resource and will perform make-up presentations for librarians who missed the meeting.

There is also the instruction performed out on the floor of the Holland reference department. As official department troubleshooters, electronic resource librarians are called when other reference librarians are having problems with a computer or database. This one-on-one aid is often the most important service that can be offered.

Electronic resource librarians are also responsible for many of the handout and instruction sheets prepared to explain how to use the variety of programs available from the Libraries.

CONCLUSION

"Reference librarianship has changed tremendously in the past 20 years."[7] The need to have reference librarians who understand, can work with, and teach new technologies is imperative. It is also important that people working in the public service departments can voice their concerns about electronic resources to those working in systems and other departments. The four electronic resource librarians at Holland Library are in positions to do just that.

As part of their official job descriptions, electronic resource librarians teach both librarians and library patrons how to use new electronic resources. They are also positioned to have regular, official and unofficial, conversations with others in non-public service departments where decisions about technology are sometimes made. Because electronic resource librarians deal regularly with new technologies, talk technology with patrons and colleagues, and keep current with pertinent manuals and articles, they can understand the unique language that accompanies this specialized field. It is important for a reference department to have individuals who can talk and understand that language.

Although these positions have an excellent potential for aiding conversation and improving decision-making processes, they have sometimes fallen short in these areas. Often, the reason has been a lack of understanding as to the responsibilities and authority given to these positions. In order for these positions to function properly, there is a great need for official recognition in job descriptions. If maintaining electronic resources is going to be a large part of a reference librarian's job, it should be described as such. In addition, clearly defined, written policies should exist for all points of technological contention such as CD-ROM purchases, LAN space distribution, who maintains what type of Web pages, and what is the function of an Electronic Resource Committee.

In today's fast-paced, technology-rich reference environments, many skills are necessary to serve as a knowledgeable librarian. The need for Electronic Resource Librarians within reference departments will only grow. This is an exciting and rewarding area of librarianship in which to work, and an area in which there will no doubt continue to be much development.

NOTES

1. "Positions Open," *American Libraries*, March 1995: 242.

2. "Positions Open," *College and Research Libraries News*, no 8 (September 1995): 593.

3. For a discussion of this electronic resource librarian's integration of GIS into Holland Reference, see Hyon-Sook (Joy) Suh and Angela Lee, "Embracing GIS Services in Libraries: The Washington State University Experience," *The Reference Librarian*, no. 64.

4. "Government CD-ROMS: From Bane to Boon," *Searcher*, Vol. 3 no. 8 (September 1996): 18-20.

5. For a discussion of the split in managing Holland's government documents, see Lou Vyhnanek, "Managing CD-ROM and Electronic Documents Sources for Holland Reference Services: The Washington State University Libraries Experience," *The Reference Librarian, no. 64*.

6. "Appendix 2, Guidelines for Resource Selection," in *Report of the WSU Libraries Task Force on Access to Electronic Resources*. Pullman, WA: WSU Libraries, 1994. Photocopied.

7. Moore, Audrey, "Reference Librarianship: It Was the Best of Times, It Was . . . ," *The Reference Librarian* no. 57 (1996): 4.

APPENDIX 1
Position Descriptions

Date: September, 1993
Incumbent: Louis Vyhnanek

POSITION DESCRIPTION

I. *Title:*   Reference Librarian and Coordinator of Humanities/
Social Sciences CD-ROM Databases

II. *Unit:*   Holland Library Public Services

III. *Position Entry Date:* 1984

IV. *Reporting Relationship:*
Reports to Head, Holland Library Public Services

V. *General Description:*
Provides general and in-depth reference service in the Humanities and
Social Sciences. Has reference and collection development responsi-
bility in American, Canadian, and Latin American History, as well as
Comparative American Cultures, which includes Black Studies, Chi-
cano Studies, Native American Studies, and Asian/Pacific American
Studies. Has overall subject responsibility in the areas of state, United
Nations, and international documents. Serves as coordinator of Hu-
manities/Social Sciences CD-ROM Databases. Responsible for any
CD-ROM problems and the setting up of new CD-ROM databases in
the Humanities/Social Sciences.

VI. *Major Responsibilities:*
  A. *Reference* (40%)
    1. Retrieves and interprets all library resources for patrons.
    2. Provides in-depth reference assistance in the fields of Ameri-
can, Canadian, and Latin American History, Comparative American Cultures, as well as state, United Nations, and international documents.
  B. *Collection Development* (20%)
    1. Evaluates the collection and orders materials in American His-
tory, Canadian History, Latin American History, and Compar-

APPENDIX 1 (continued)

ative American Cultures. Has collection responsibility for state, United Nations, and international documents.

2. Acts as liaison between the library and the American History, Canadian History, Latin American History, and Comparative American Cultures faculty, trying to be responsive to their concerns about the library collections and keeping them informed about library collection policies and budgetary limitations.

C. *Coordinating CD-ROM Databases* (30%)
   1. Serves as the resource person for all the CD-ROM products available in the Humanities/Social Sciences.
   2. Works with subject specialists in each area in becoming expert in using each of the CD-ROMs.
   3. Provides regular instruction to all Holland Library reference librarians and users in CD-ROM searching, retrieval, and general operation.
   4. Responsible for any hardware or software problems, informing the librarians about new developments, and setting up new CD-ROM databases.

D. *Library and University Service* (5%)
   1. Participates regularly in recruitment and selection of faculty.
   2. Serves on library committees and task forces.
   3. Serves on university committees.
   4. Participates in library instruction and orientation activities, including general tours.
   5. Does presentations for classes in History and Comparative American Cultures subject areas.

E. *Professional Scholarly Activities* (5%)
   1. Devotes professional time (within and outside of the work week) to keeping abreast of trends and developments in the fields of library and information science and higher education by reading professional literature, participating in professional organizations and attending workshops, institutes, etc., at the local, state, regional, and national levels, and completing other scholarly activities for professional development such as presentation of papers, research and publication, etc.
   2. Shares with other division and library personnel relevant information obtained from professional activities and when ap-

propriate uses knowledge gained to evaluate and improve library services.

Date: October, 1996
Incumbent: Louis Vyhnanek

POSITION DESCRIPTION

I. *Title*:   Reference Librarian and Electronic Resources Librarian, Social Sciences

II. *Unit*:   Holland Library Public Services

III. *Position Entry Date*: 1984

IV. *Reporting Relationship:*
Reports to Head, Holland Library Public Services

V. *General Description:*
Provides general and in-depth reference service in the Humanities and Social Sciences. Has reference and collection development responsibility in American, Canadian, and Latin American History, as well as Comparative American Cultures, which includes African American Studies, Chicano Studies, Native American Studies, and Asian/Pacific American Studies. Has overall subject responsibility in the areas of state, United Nations, and international documents. Serves as Electronic Resources Librarian for the Social Sciences. Responsible for any documents CD-ROM problems and the setting up of new government CD-ROM databases in the Humanities/Social Sciences.

VI. *Major Responsibilities:*

A. *Reference* (35%)
1. Retrieves and interprets all library resources for patrons.
2. Provides in-depth reference assistance in the fields of American, Canadian, and Latin American History, Comparative American Cultures, as well as state, United Nations, and international documents.

B. *Collection Development* (20%)
1. Evaluates the collection and orders materials in American History, Canadian History, Latin American History, and Comparative American Cultures. Has collection responsibility for state, United Nations, and international documents.

APPENDIX 1 (continued)

2. Acts as liaison between the library and the American History, Canadian History, Latin American History, and Comparative American Cultures faculty, trying to be responsive to their concerns about the library collections and keeping them informed about library collection policies and budgetary limitations.

C. *Electronic Resources Librarian, Social Sciences* (35%)

1. Serves as the person working with the subject specialists in the Social Sciences, making them aware of the resources available in their areas through the Internet, including listservs, Gophers, WAIS, NETSCAPE, and the World Wide Web, as well as helping them access data through these locations.
2. Keeps up with the latest developments and strategies in accessing material through the Internet and serves as liaison with the Information Technology Help Desk and the systems Office for questions about electronic resources in the Social Sciences.
3. Responsible for any hardware or software problems involving electronic and CD-ROM databases in the areas of state and international documents.

D. *Library and University Service* (5%)

1. Participates regularly in recruitment and selection of faculty.
2. Serves on library committees and task forces.
3. Serves on university committees.
4. Participates in library instruction and orientation activities, including general tours.
5. Does presentations for classes in History and Comparative American Cultures subject areas.

E. *Professional Scholarly Activities* (5%)

1. Devotes professional time (within and outside of the work week) to keeping abreast of trends and developments in the fields of library and information science and higher education by reading professional literature, participating in professional organizations and attending workshops, institutes, etc., at the local, state, regional, and national levels, and completing other scholarly activities for professional development such as presentation of papers, research and publication, etc.
2. Shares with other division and library personnel relevant information obtained from professional activities and when ap-

propriate uses knowledge gained to evaluate and improve library services.

Date: June 1995
Incumbent: B. Jane Scales

POSITION DESCRIPTION

I. *Title*:   Reference Librarian, Slavic Bibliographer, and Electronic Resources Librarian, Humanities

II. *Unit*:   Holland Library Public Services

III. *Position Entry Date*: 1992, revised 1995.

IV. *Reporting Relationship:*
Reports to Head, Holland Library Public Services

V. *General Description:*
Provides general and in-depth reference service in the Humanities and Social Sciences. Has reference and collection development responsibility in Slavic Languages and Literatures, German Language and Literature, and Library and Information Science. Serves as Electronic Resources Librarian for the Humanities. Responsible for any non-Government document CD-ROM problems and the setting up of new non-government document CD-ROM databases in the Humanities/Social Sciences.

VI. *Major Responsibilities:*
A. *Reference* (35%)
   1. Retrieves and interprets all library resources for patrons.
   2. Provides in-depth reference assistance in the fields of Slavic Languages and Literature, German Language and Literature, and Library and Information Science.

B. *Electronic Resources Librarian, Humanities* (25%)
   1. Serves as the person working with the subject specialists in the Humanities, making them aware of the resources available in their areas through the Internet, including listservs, Gophers, WAIS, MOSAIC, and the World Wide Web, as well as helping them access data through these locations.

APPENDIX 1 (continued)

2. Keeps up with the latest developments and strategies in accessing material through the Internet and serves as liaison with the Information Technology Help Desk and the Systems Office for questions about electronic resources in the Humanities.
3. Responsible for any hardware or software problems involving non-government document CD-ROM databases, keeping the other librarians aware of any new developments, and setting up new CD-ROM databases in this area.

C. *Collection Development (20%)*
1. Evaluates the collection and orders materials in Slavic Languages and Literatures, German Language and Literature, and Library and Information Science.
2. Acts as liaison between the library and the German Language faculty and Russian Language faculty, trying to be responsive to their concerns about the library collections and keeping them informed about library collection policies and budgetary limitations.

D. *Supervises Microforms Section (10%)*
1. Hires and schedules time-slip employees for section. Conducts personnel disciplinary actions and termination if needed.
2. Supervises Library Technician Lead assigned to section. Conducts annual review.
3. Prepares annual time-slip budget request.
4. Submits annual equipment request list if needed.

E. *Library and University Service (5%)*
1. Participates regularly in recruitment and selection of faculty.
2. Serves on library committees and task forces.
3. Serves on university committees.
4. Participates in library instruction and orientation activities, including general tours.
5. Does presentations for classes in German and Russian literature subject areas.

F. *Professional Scholarly Activities (5%)*
1. Devotes professional time (within and outside of the work week) to keeping abreast of trends and developments in the fields of library and information science and higher education

by reading professional literature, participating in professional organizations and attending workshops, institutes, etc., at the local, state, regional, and national levels, and completing other scholarly activities for professional development such as presentation of papers, research and publication, etc.

2. Shares with other division and library personnel relevant information obtained from professional activities and when appropriate uses knowledge gained to evaluate and improve library services.

Date: August 1997
Incumbent: B. Jane Scales

POSITION DESCRIPTION

I. *Title*:   Reference/Electronic Resources Librarian

II. *Unit*:   Holland Library Public Services

III. *Position Entry Date*: 1992, revised 1995, 1997.

IV. *Reporting Relationship:*
Reports to Head, Holland Library Public Services

V. *General Description:*
- General and in-depth reference service in the Humanities and Social Sciences.
- Reference and collection development responsibility in Slavic Languages and Literatures.
- German Language and Literature, and Library and Information Science.
- Electronic Resources Librarian for the Humanities, responsible for any non-Government document CD-ROM problems and the setting up of new non-government document CD-ROM databases in the Humanities/Social Sciences.
- Coordinates library services for Extended Degree Students, and serves as course developer and instructor for University 300 course.

VI. *Major Responsibilities:*
   A. *Reference* (30%)

APPENDIX 1 (continued)

1. Assists library users in retrieving and interpreting library resources in Humanities, Social Sciences, and Government Documents.
2. Provides in-depth reference assistance in the fields of Slavic Languages and Literature, German Language and Literature, Library and Information Science, and Electronic Resources.

B. *Library User Education* (20%)

1. Serves as Univ300 course instructor, maintains course material including course guide book and Web modules.
2. Teaches instructional sessions as needed, concentrating on Internet resource retrieval and electronic resources such as Lexis-Nexis.
3. Contributes to other electronic-oriented User Education projects as needed.

C. *Extended Degree Library Support* (10%)

1. Supervises one 50% FTE staff and coordinates library services for students in the Washington State University Extended Degree Program.

D. *Electronic Resources* (15%)

1. Works with the subject specialists in both the Humanities and Social Sciences, to implement networked electronic resources in coordination with the WSU Libraries' Systems office.
2. Keeps up with the latest developments and strategies in accessing material through the Internet and serves as liaison with the Information Technology Student Computing Services and the Libraries' Systems Office for questions about non-government document electronic resources.
3. Responsible for any hardware or software problems involving non-government document CD-ROM databases, keeping the other librarians aware of any new developments, and setting up new CD-ROM databases in this area.

E. *Collection Development* (5%)

1. Evaluates the collection and orders materials in Slavic Languages and Literatures, German Language and Literature, and Library and Information Science.
2. Acts as liaison between the library and the German Language faculty and Russian Language faculty, being responsive to

their concerns about the library collections and keeping them informed about library collection policies and budgetary limitations.

F. *Library and University Service* (10%)
1. Serves on library committees and task forces.
2. Serves on university committees.
3. Participates regularly in recruitment and selection of faculty.
4. Participates in library instruction and orientation activities, including general tours.

G. *Professional Scholarly Activities* (10%)
1. Devotes professional time (within and outside of the work week) to keeping abreast of trends and developments in the fields of library and information science and higher education by reading professional literature, participating in professional organizations and attending workshops, institutes, etc., at the local, state, regional, and national levels, and completing other scholarly activities for professional development such as presentation of papers, research and publication, etc.
2. Shares with other division and library personnel relevant information obtained from professional activities and when appropriate uses knowledge gained to evaluate and improve library services.

Position Description
SOCIAL SCIENCE REFERENCE AND ELECTRONIC RESOURCE LIBRARIAN
Humanities/Social Sciences Libraries

Elizabeth Felt
August 9, 1995

I. *BRIEF DESCRIPTION:*

Serve in the capacity of reference librarian with responsibility for general and in-depth reference service, collection development responsibilities in designated subject areas, faculty liaison duties with designated departments and user education instruction and orientation, and electronic resource development and maintenance responsibilities. Includes night and/or weekend reference shifts. Also, coordinate the Information Assistants.

APPENDIX 1 (continued)

II. *REPORTING RELATIONSHIP:*

Report to the Head, Humanities/Social Sciences Libraries. Work closely with other reference librarians, with the Head of Holland Reference,
and with the Social Sciences Collection Development Coordinator.

III. *MAJOR RESPONSIBILITIES:*

A. *Reference Services* (35%)
   1. Provide reference assistance to library users both on and off the
      reference desk, utilizing both traditional and electronic sources.
   2. Provide comprehensive reference assistance in the fields of
      subject specialization.
   3. Participate in weekly reference department meetings; make
      recommendations for reference collection development in as-
      signed subject areas.
   4. Regularly review new reference titles and occasionally update
      knowledge of older parts of the reference collection.
   5. May participate in other reference activities such as the record-
      ing of statistics, task forces, orienting new librarians in refer-
      ence sources in subject areas of expertise.

B. *Information Assistants Program* (10%)
   1. Hire, train, schedule, and supervise all graduate students who
      serve as Information Assistants.
   2. Monitor the budget for Information Assistants.
   3. Train, schedule and coordinate all library staff who serve as
      Information Assistants.
   4. Coordinate the Information Assistant schedule with the Head
      of Holland Reference.

C. *Collection Development and Departmental Liaison* (10%)
   1. Responsible for selection, evaluation, and weeding of library
      materials in designated subject areas.
   2. Serve as librarian liaison to designated program/departments.
      Meet with new faculty and become familiar with research
      interests of faculty members.
   3. In cooperation with the Social Sciences Collection Develop-
      ment Head, write and revise collection development policies
      in designated subject areas.
   4. Participate in collection analysis projects when pertinent.

D. *User Education* (10%)
1. Participate in general library instruction sessions for various classes, as needed.
2. As part of library liaison responsibilities, conduct instruction sessions for classes in designated departments. May be called upon to assist with other classes.
3. May produce instructional materials for use in any of the activities mentioned above.
4. Conduct general orientation of the library as needed.
5. May participate in other user education activities such as faculty seminars, database seminars, etc.

E. *Electronic Resources* (5%)
1. Develop and maintain various portions of the WSU Libraries Home Page.
2. Teach classes on the use of computer applications and electronic resources.
3. Member of WWW Subcommittee of DCIC.
4. Back-up for social science, humanities, and government documents CD-ROM.
5. Work with other electronic resource librarians in the exploration and implementation of new information technologies for the Libraries.

F. *Professional/Scholarly Activities* (20%)
1. Devote professional time (within and outside the work week) to keeping abreast of trends and developments in the fields of library and information science, higher education, and management by reading professional literature and participating in appropriate listservs, etc.
2. Participate in professional organizations and attend workshops, conferences, institutes, etc., at the local, state, and national levels.
3. Complete other scholarly activities for professional development such as scholarly presentations of papers, research and publications, etc.
4. Share with other division and library personnel relevant information obtained from professional activities and, when appropriate, use knowledge gained to evaluate and improve library services.

APPENDIX 1 (continued)

G. *Service* (10%)
  1. Serve on library committees, task forces, etc.
  2. Serve on university committees, task forces, etc.
  3. Perform related special assignments as necessary.

NB:NW
K:felt

Position Description
SOCIAL SCIENCE REFERENCE AND ELECTRONIC RESOURCE LIBRARIAN
Humanities/Social Sciences Libraries

Elizabeth Felt
September 30, 1997

I. *BRIEF DESCRIPTION:*

Serve in the capacity of reference librarian with responsibility for general and in-depth reference service, collection development responsibilities in designated subject areas, faculty liaison duties with designated departments and user education instruction and orientation, and electronic resource development and maintenance responsibilities. Includes night and/or weekend reference shifts.

II. *REPORTING RELATIONSHIP:*

Report to the Head, Humanities/Social Sciences Libraries. Work closely with other reference librarians, with the Head of Holland Reference, and with the Social Sciences Collection Development Coordinator.

III. *MAJOR RESPONSIBILITIES:*

A. *Reference Services* (30%)
  1. Provide reference assistance to library users both on and off the reference desk, utilizing both traditional and electronic sources.
  2. Provide comprehensive reference assistance in the fields of subject specialization.
  3. Participate in weekly reference department meetings; make

recommendations for reference collection development in assigned subject areas.

4. Regularly review new reference titles and occasionally update knowledge of older parts of the reference collection.
5. May participate in other reference activities such as the recording of statistics, task forces, orienting new librarians in reference sources in subject areas of expertise.

B. *Collection Development and Departmental Liaison* (25%)

1. Responsible for selection, evaluation, and weeding of library materials in designated subject areas.
2. Serve as librarian liaison to designated program/departments. Meet with faculty and become familiar with research interests of faculty members.
3. In cooperation with the Social Sciences Collection Development Head, write and revise collection development policies in designated subject areas.
4. Participate in collection analysis projects when pertinent.

C. *User Education* (10%)

1. Participate in general library instruction sessions for various classes, as needed.
2. As part of library liaison responsibilities, conduct instruction sessions for classes in designated departments. May be called upon to assist with other classes.
3. May produce instructional materials for use in any of the activities mentioned above.
4. Conduct general orientation of the library as needed.
5. May participate in other user education activities such as faculty seminars, database seminars, etc.

D. *Electronic Resources* (15%)

1. Develop and maintain various portions of the WSU Libraries Home Page.
2. Teach classes on the use of computer applications and electronic resources.
3. Member of WWW Subcommittee of DCIC.
4. Member of Electronic Resources Committee.
5. Member of DCIC.
6. Back-up for social science, humanities, and government documents CD-ROMs.

APPENDIX 1 (continued)

7. Work with other electronic resource librarians in the exploration and implementation of new information technologies for the Libraries.

E. *Professional/Scholarly Activities* (10%)
  1. Devote professional time (within and outside the work week) to keeping abreast of trends and developments in the fields of library and information science, higher education, and management by reading professional literature and participating in appropriate listservs, etc.
  2. Participate in professional organizations and attend workshops, conferences, institutes, etc. at the local, state, and national levels.
  3. Complete other scholarly activities for professional development such as scholarly presentations of papers, research and publications, etc.
  4. Share with other division and library personnel relevant information obtained from professional activities and, when appropriate, use knowledge gained to evaluate and improve library services.

F. *Service* (10%)
  1. Serve on library committees, task forces, etc.
  2. Serve on university committees, task forces, etc.
  3. Perform related special assignments as necessary.

1996

POSITION DESCRIPTION

POSITION TITLE: Government Publications/Datafiles Librarian

APPOINTMENT LEVEL: 1.00 FTE, Annual

I. OVERALL BRIEF DESCRIPTION:

Description: Oversees the U.S. and Washington State depository programs, coordinates collection development for state, regional, federal and international documents, serves as the WSU Liaison to the Inter-University Consortium for Political and Social Research (ICPSR); provides general and specialized reference service and user education in Holland/New Library.

Duties: Liaison with ICPSR, U.S. Depository Program, and other governmental agencies; instruction in library use; reference service using printed and electronic resources.

II. *REPORTING RELATIONSHIPS:*

Reports to the Head, Humanities/Social Science Libraries. Works closely with other reference librarians throughout the library system, the Head of Library User Education, and Head of Bibliographic Control.

III. *MAJOR RESPONSIBILITIES:*

A. *Liaison and Collection Development Responsibility* (20%)
1. Serves as the WSU liaison to the U.S. Government Depository Program and insures that WSU Libraries are meeting depository requirements.
2. Serves as the liaison to state and international agencies for publications appropriate to the collections.
3. Works closely with the staff in Bibliographic Control (who process government publications), staff in Circulation (who maintain the collections), and Media Material Services and Information Technology (for ICPSR tapes and other resources in electronic format) to insure that documents and datafiles are processed according to contractual responsibility and are readily accessible to the public.
4. Works with the reference librarians selectors to identify and acquire the appropriate state, federal, and international publications.

B. *Reference* (35%)
1. Serves as a resource for state, federal, and international government publications.
2. Provides comprehensive reference assistance to library users, utilizing reference sources in a wide variety of formats; includes some evening and weekend duties.
3. Participates in the development of reference policies, makes recommendations for reference collection development in assigned subject areas.
4. Assists in special projects to improve organization and access to materials and services with the Holland Library.

APPENDIX 1 (continued)

C. *Library User Education* (15%)
1. Teaches classes and workshops in the use of government publications and ICPSR tapes either separately or in partnership with other reference librarian liaisons to specific academic departments and faculty in the social sciences.
2. Teaches general library instruction sessions.
3. Teaches and/or participates in Library User Education seminars such as Internet training.
4. Produces instructional materials as needed.

D. *Professional/Scholarly/Creative Activity and Library Service* (30%)
1. Participates in library and university planning by serving on library and campus committees, task forces, etc.
2. Participates in the library profession on a regional and national basis.
3. Keeps abreast of trends in librarianship, information technology, and higher education.
4. Conducts research and publishes results.
5. Performs related special assignments as necessary.

E. *Other duties as assigned*

_____

Incumbent's signature

_____

Head, Humanities/Social Sciences Libraries

1997

POSITION DESCRIPTION

POSITION TITLE: Government Publications and GIS Coordinator

APPOINTMENT LEVEL: 1.00 FTE, Annual

I. *OVERALL BRIEF DESCRIPTION:*

Oversees Collection Management and Electronic Resources for U.S. Government Publications. Coordinates Libraries GIS and geospatial data applications. Serves as the WSU Liaison to the U.S. Government

Depository Program and one of the WSU Liaisons to the Inter-University Consortium for Political and Social Research (ICPSR). Serves as Electronic Resources Librarian for the Social Sciences. Provides general and specialized reference service involving documents and GIS and user education in Holland/New Library.

II. *REPORTING RELATIONSHIPS:*

Reports to the Head, Humanities/Social Sciences Libraries. Works closely with other reference librarians throughout the library system, the Head of Media Materials Services, the Head of Library User Education, and Head of Bibliographic Control.

III. *MAJOR RESPONSIBILITIES:*

A. Liaison and Collection Development Responsibility (15%)

1. Serves as the WSU liaison to the U.S. Government Depository Program and insures that WSU Libraries are meeting depository requirement.
2. Works closely with the staff in Bibliographic Control (who process government documents) and Media Material Services and Information Technology to insure that documents and datafiles are processed according to contractual responsibility and are readily accessible to the public.
3. Works with the reference librarian selectors to identify and acquire the appropriate U.S. government publications.

B. *Reference* (40%)

1. Serves as a resource person for the U.S. government publications and geospatial data (GIS).
2. Provide comprehensive reference assistance to library users in all formats.
3. Participates in the development of reference policies, make recommendations for reference collection development in the U.S. government publications and other electronic resources for the social sciences.
4. Assists in special projects to improve access to materials and services in Holland/New Library.

C. Electronic Resources (25-30%)

1. Serves as the primary person to maintain the U.S government databases including online resources and CD-ROMs loaded on the documents workstations (currently two) and LAN in Holland/New Library.

APPENDIX 1 (continued)

2. Serves as the primary person to maintain datafiles loaded on the GIS machine in the terminal room in Holland/New Library.
3. Assists in acquiring electronic resources for the social sciences by following the procedures indicated in the *Guidelines for Selecting, Processing, and Accessing Electronic Resources* (AEIOU).
4. Participates in trouble shooting problems with computer equipment and planning for future use of electronic resources and purchasing equipment.

D. *Library User Education* (5-10%)
  1. Teaches classes and workshops in the use of government publications and GIS software either separately, or in partnership with other reference librarian liaisons, to library faculty and staff and/or to specific departments in the social sciences.
  2. Participates in teaching general library instruction session (e.g., Eng. 101)
  3. Produces instructional materials as needed.
  4. Participates in Library User Education seminars such as Internet Training.

E. *Professional and Library Services* (20%)
  1. Participates in library and university committees and task forces.
  2. Participates in the library profession on a regional and national basis.
  3. Conducts research and publishes results.
  4. Keeps up with new trends in information technology, librarianship, and higher education.

F. *Other duties assigned*

10/97/Suh

APPENDIX 2
Task Force Report

GUIDELINES FOR ELECTRONIC RESOURCE SELECTION

GENERAL CRITERIA:

Electronic resources purchased or leased by WSU Libraries should meet the criteria listed below. [These criteria are not in priority order.]

A. *Content*
1. The information content should be relevant to the information needs of the WSU community. Electronic resources of central importance (core) to a given discipline will generally be given priority in selection. Departments and programs that will benefit from acquisition of the database should be identified.
2. The coverage must be comparable or superior to other electronic or print products which cover the same materials, if any. [Example: Periodical Abstracts on CD-ROM might be selected over Reader's Guide because it has broader coverage for the same price, if other factors were comparable.]
3. The electronic resource should have a significant amount of material that is not already covered by other resources leased or owned [the term "lease" in this document refers to any electronic resource that WSU Libraries does not own, but pays fees to access via the internet, OCLC, DIALOG, other on-line services, or CD-ROM products]. If another version/format currently exists in the collection a cancellation recommendation should be made by the appropriate subject librarian (see criteria 9 for details) or key decision makers (document to be attached).
4. The accuracy and completeness of information in the electronic resource should be verified by a librarian.
5. Bibliographic databases must be updated at least on an annual basis. All electronic resources should have an update frequency that reflects the nature of the data and needs of users. [For directories, once a year may be sufficient, but for current awareness resources it is not.]
6. Non-bibliographic/media resources should be selected using the same criteria stated in the collection development policy statements used for print materials.

APPENDIX 2 (continued)

B. *Software*

    7. The software should be "user friendly," as determined by the presence of these criteria (below). In addition, the electronic version should also be at least as easy to use as the printed version, if one exists.

- Search engines should be appropriate to the material. If similar products are available, those offering more than one search capability may be preferable.
- Free-text and index/thesaurus searching are both available.
- Boolean, proximity and truncated searches are all desirable.
- Retrieval speed is fast.
- Search strategies can be saved and rerun.
- Control over how records are displayed and output is desirable.
- Both printing and download of records is possible.
- The display is visually appealing and distinguishes between record elements.
- On-screen help and error messages are clear and context sensitive.
- The software is compatible with existing hardware, especially memory requirements, and can be networked.
- Installation and updating is relatively easy.

In regard to non-bibliographic/media resources, the above criteria may apply as well as the following:

- Hypertext is desirable.
- For full text resources, adjacency, numerical operators, and relevancy are desirable.

    8. An attempt will be made to keep the number of different search software packages that staff and patrons must learn to a minimum. If different vendors offer the same electronic resource, preference will be given to vendors from whom we already purchase other databases.

C. *Cost*

    9. The cost must be competitive with other comparable electronic versions of the information, if any. Cost calculations should include:

- Costs per use on an annual basis.
- Back files to be purchased, if any.
- Network fees.
- Discounts for concurrent print/microfiche subscriptions.
- Estimates of new and ongoing associated hardware costs.
- Estimates of costs related to increased demands on technical support staff and user training (other staff).
- Potential savings from the cancellation of other formats.
- Costs of competing products, if any, for comparison.
- Cost of necessary software, if not included.

10. Maintaining a resource in multiple formats must be justified by the appropriate subject librarian or key decision makers (document to be attached). For instance, any of the following factors could be justification for keeping both print and electronic formats:
    - The electronic version has no archival coverage.
    - The information content is different between formats.
    - The licensing agreement restricts downloading or printing.
    - Multiple user access to the electronic version is inadequate to meet user demands.
    - Graphic or other visual features are in print, but not in electronic format.

11. If a comparable or superior product is freely available on a network from a reliable source outside WSU, a new product will not be added unless:
    - There is little or no cost associated with its addition.
    - An exception should be made based on factors in sections 10 or 21.
    - A cooperative collection development agreement with another institution to provide access would be violated. [Example: WSU's agreement with the University of Idaho Library.]
    - Better on-campus access can be provided.

D. *Networkability*

12. If at all possible, core electronic resources should meet campus networking standards even if financial and/or legal limitations prevent networking immediately.

13. For comparable (quality, cost, etc.) electronic resources, pref-

APPENDIX 2 (continued)

erence will be given to those products for which there is no charge for networking.

14. Lease or license agreements which allow multiple, simultaneous users, including dial-in access, are preferable if cost limitations can also be met.

15. Any software or hardware required to use the resource should be compatible with our current (and anticipated future) network hardware and software. The organization of data should conform with international standards.

E. *Leveraging Existing Resources and Services*

16. Electronic resources should enhance access to existing WSU resources and services, regardless of format.
    - The resource should enhance access to materials in WSU collections which are currently inaccessible.
    - The resource should provide improved access to journals owned by WSU or conveniently available through cooperative agreements. [For example, ARIEL.]
    - Electronic resources should maximize usage of existing resources and services, including library staff, technical support, equipment, systems, print/downloading capabilities, etc.

F. *Additional Considerations*

17. The anticipated usage of the electronic resource should be significant relative to cost, but should not be an overriding factor for core resources.

18. For comparable (quality, cost, etc.) electronic resources, preference will be given to those products which we own as opposed to those we lease.

19. Increased demands on library staff (reference, user education, interlibrary loan, technical support) should be estimated and must be in proportion to the cost and importance of the resource.

20. A sample version or remote access trial period should be arranged for new resources before purchase so that librarians

and other interested faculty and students can review the product. In addition, product reviews or current users, if available, should be consulted before purchase.

21. Non-core electronic resources may be purchased if they meet one of the following criteria:
    a. They allow for improved service to users by making it easier for librarians and staff to perform their duties.
    b. They will replace large volumes of low usage material that is taking up a significant amount of needed space and/or requires too much time to maintain in an existing format.
    c. They provide unique access for users' needs and are inexpensive.
22. Requests by departments, faculty or staff to purchase electronic resources should meet most of the above criteria.

ACCESS/OWNERSHIP CONSIDERATIONS

The relative value of ownership versus providing access must be weighed against institutional needs. Options available may be CD-ROM, floppy disk, remote database services or other remote resources. Points to consider are:
1. Local control or ownership is desired for various reasons including the need to archive the resource.
2. Superior interface capabilities are available in one of these options.
3. Frequent updates are needed, as in current awareness services, and may only be available with one of the options.
4. The resource is cost effective based on cost of subscription, use, hardware, software, networking, technical support, etc. (see section 9)

POST-SELECTION EVALUATION

Once an electronic resource has been made available, it should be evaluated periodically by appropriate individuals, such as subject specialists and/or users, where appropriate, and/or a collections coordinating group and/or Information Technology and/or consortium.
1. Comparison of different versions of the resource to assess completeness and currency.

APPENDIX 2 (continued)

2. Analysis of simultaneous user needs, including acceptable response time.
3. Assessment of use statistics.
4. Evaluation of vendor responsiveness.
5. Analysis of price increases or network licensing policy changes.
6. Evaluation of the content and frequency of users' comments.
7. Determination if a superior product is now available.

MN/EB
4/18/94 rev 4/28 EB

APPENDIX 3
Untitled, Pre-Purchase Responsibilities/
Post-Purchase Responsibilities

Because the Report of the Task Force on Access to Electronic Resources was written before the establishment of "Electronic Resource Librarians" in the Hum/Soc Unit, those of us who have assumed this title and its implications feel a review of the report by the Unit is warranted to better facilitate the selection, purchase, use, and maintenance of electronic resources (especially CD-ROMs) in Holland Reference, and to clarify the roles and responsibilities of both collection developers and Electronic Resources Librarians.

Pre-Purchase Responsibilities

Collection Developers:

1. Gather information on products, alternative companies as completely as possible, including product and company names, and phone numbers.
2. Provide additional information necessary to facilitate the decision making process–i.e., product reviews, listserv comments, etc.
3. Provide input on product evaluation.

Electronic Resources Librarians:

1. Contact companies to arrange test products, or temporary access to products.

2. Assess qualities of products produced by various vendors.
3. Work with Systems Office to determine appropriateness of software and hardware requirements as they coincide/clash with current hardware and software configurations in the Library.
4. Determine which workstation would best suit CD-ROM, or if possible, how the CD-ROM could be placed on the LAN.
5. Consult with collection developer on these criteria.

Post-Purchase Responsibilities

Electronic Resources Librarians:

1. Facilitate installation of CD-ROM product by working with Systems (if necessary).
2. Update documentation of Electronic Resources available in the library.

Collection Developers:

1. Organization and creation (if necessary) of any help sheets or manuals pertaining to the use of the product.

Both:

- Periodically evaluate CD-ROM usefulness, and check to see if better products have come out since its purchase.

APPENDIX 4
World Wide Web Subcommittee
of DCIC

World Wide Web Subcommittee of DCIC

COMPOSITION:

The subcommittee membership includes: all electronic resource librarians; representatives from TSD, ILL, MASC, MMS, User Education; the Information Technology Librarian; the Systems Technician who works with the Web Server. The Chair of the Subcommittee functions as the Webmaster to the Library Home Pages.

APPENDIX 4 (continued)

FUNCTIONS:

The Subcommittee represents the Libraries expertise in regard to Web design, structure and maintenance. As such, the Subcommittee is responsible for the development and maintenance of all Library Web Pages. The Subcommittee determines format decisions as they pertain to public access. The Subcommittee works in conjunction with DCIC and the OPAC Subcommittee concerning Web interfaces to catalogs, indexes, and other services that the Libraries may purchase. The Subcommittee works in conjunction with collection development specialists and the CDC, who decide what types of materials should be present and available through the Libraries.

MEETINGS:

The Subcommittee meets one time each month during the school year, and as needed during the summer.

REPORTS TO:

The Subcommittee reports to DCIC. The chair of the Subcommittee is a member of DCIC.

Managing CD-ROM and Electronic Documents Sources for Holland Reference Services: The Washington State University Libraries Experience

Lou Vyhnanek

SUMMARY. The author details the evolution of the management of CD-ROM and electronic documents for reference services in the Holland/New Library (Holland), the main library at Washington State University, for the humanities and social sciences. From the arrival of the first major United States document CD-ROM disk, the *National Trade Data Bank,* the management of these CD-ROMs is presented in four phases: placing CD-ROMs on reserve in Holland circulation for use in a single drive government documents workstation; utilizing a Pioneer multi-disk changer that holds a cartridge with spaces for six CD-ROM disks, each running off a separate drive in a new-and-improved workstation; abandoning the cartridges but adding a cabinet for government CD-ROMs and a user-friendly, Auto Menu software system in yet another new-and-improved workstation; and, keeping the last configuration but sending CD-ROMs in need of special software to the Libraries' media collection and networking some government CD-ROMs over the Libraries' LAN. The Holland reference experience demonstrates that government CD-ROMs have exploded in number and grown complex in content, dictating new approaches in handling these

Lou Vyhnanek is Head, Humanities/Social Sciences Reference, Holland/New Library, Room 120F, Pullman, WA 99164-5610 (E-mail: louv@wsu.edu).

[Haworth co-indexing entry note]: "Managing CD-ROM and Electronic Documents Sources for Holland Reference Services: The Washington State University Libraries Experience." Vyhnanek, Lou. Co-published simultaneously in *The Reference Librarian* (The Haworth Press, Inc.) No. 64, 1999, pp. 113-124; and: *Coming of Age in Reference Services: A Case History of the Washington State University Libraries* (ed: Christy Zlatos) The Haworth Press, Inc., 1999, pp. 113-124. Single or multiple copies of this article are available for a fee from The Haworth Document Delivery Service [1-800-342-9678, 9:00 a.m. - 5:00 p.m. (EST). E-mail address: getinfo@haworthpressinc.com].

113

items. Librarians must continue to be willing to develop the necessary skills to explore future technologies to access information in these new formats. *[Article copies available for a fee from The Haworth Document Delivery Service: 1-800-342-9678. E-mail address: getinfo@haworthpressinc.com]*

This article focuses on the evolution of the management of CD-ROM and electronic documents for reference services in the Holland/ New Library (Holland), the main library at Washington State University, for the humanities and social sciences. The present situation had its beginnings more than seven years ago (late 1990), with the arrival of the first major United States document CD-ROM disk, the *National Trade Data Bank*. Electronic documents reference services have since grown into providing access to 200 CD-ROM disks in the Holland Library alone, with many more in other locations, running under a variety of different software, as well as locating government information electronically on the Internet through databases such as GPO Access and STAT-USA. This situation is not unique to WSU Libraries. It is similar to that faced by any large depository library throughout the United States, which has had to deal with this explosion of CD-ROMs and electronic resources.

INTRODUCTION AND BACKGROUND

Before tracing the history of providing access to these resources at Holland Library, it is necessary to give some background on how United States government documents are processed at the Washington State University Libraries. The Libraries do not have a separate government documents department, where all federal documents are processed and made available to the public in one location. As a member of the Federal Depository Library Program, the Libraries receive 65% of all the items sent through this program. Depository items sent to the Libraries first arrive in the Documents Processing Unit, a part of the Technical Services Division. From there, the documents are processed and sent to the shelves of the appropriate library where those subject resources are located. For example, United States documents in both paper and microfiche in the humanities/social sciences are located in Holland Library; those whose subject matter falls within the sciences are housed in the Owen Science and Engineering Library (Owen).

There are several branch libraries within the Libraries (including the Brain Education Library, the Veterinary Medical/Pharmacy Library, the Architecture Library, and the Fischer Agricultural Sciences Library) that have some government documents, but Holland and Owen have by far the largest number of United States documents in their collections.

Until recently, this same division given to the documents collection also has been applied to the United States government CD-ROMs. Those CD-ROMs with subject matter in the humanities/social sciences were located at Holland; those in the sciences were located in Owen. This remained the way things were handled until 1995, when all of the science document CD-ROMs and a small percentage of Holland's were moved to Media Materials Services, located in the Holland/New Library building, and merged with the Libraries' media collection. Within the Holland/New Library, most of the CD-ROMs are located in Holland Reference; only those requiring special software are located in Media Materials Services.

In terms of the documents situation within the Libraries, documents processing and the reference or public services function for documents have been two separate operations. As of 1996, there was one Holland Social Sciences Reference Librarian (Mary Gilles) with public services responsibility for United States documents, both print and microfiche. This librarian served as the liaison for these materials with the faculty and staff in the Documents Processing Unit (Margot Krissiep, and more recently, Phyllis Ritter) and the staff in the Documents Serial Record Unit (Linda Crane and Susan Ferguson), who process document serials. As of 1996, there was also one Holland Social Sciences Reference Librarian (Lou Vyhnanek) with liaison responsibility for United States document CD-ROMs. This involved working with the documents processing staff noted above and also the Libraries' Systems Office staff to insure that the documents CD-ROMs were processed in a timely manner and set up in a location where they were made available for public use.

SITUATION IN THE ORIGINAL HOLLAND LIBRARY BUILDING

In late 1990 and early 1991, WSU Libraries began to receive the first United States government document CD-ROMs. At first, there were only a few individual titles, but with the government's decision to put a large portion of the data from the *1990 Census of Population and Housing* on CD-ROM, as well as a number of individual agencies putting more and more material on disk, the number of CD-ROM disks available quickly began to grow. This led to the need for a decision as to where those disks cataloged for Holland were to be located.

For three years (from the time when the first CD-ROM disks were received until the move to the New Library addition in May 1994), Holland (humanities/social sciences) reference was located in the original Holland Library building, which was built in 1950. The initial decision was to make United States documents CD-ROMs available for use at a public workstation in the reference area. Problems soon developed because Holland reference's computer workstations only had single CD-ROM drives, either as separate units or as units built into the workstations. This meant that only one CD-ROM disk at a time could be used at a terminal. With the growing number of government titles on CD-ROM, a place had to be found for storing the disks near the computer.

The first solution to this problem was to place all the United States documents CD-ROMs on reserve at the Holland circulation desk. After checking out a disk from reserve for two hours, patrons could take the disk, which was stored in a jewel case to protect it, across the hall to Holland reference and load it into a caddy or container that was then placed in the CD-ROM drive. When the patron was through accessing the material on the disk, she placed the disk back into the jewel case and returned it to the reserve desk.

This solution worked for awhile but, as more and more disks began coming in this format, there was a need to provide a location for the disks closer to the workstation. Discussions between the liaison for United States government documents CD-ROMS (Lou Vyhnanek) and the then Assistant Systems Librarian (Craig Summerhill) led to the purchasing of a Pioneer multi-disk changer for a separate government documents workstation. The multi-disk changer could hold a cartridge that had spaces for six CD-ROM disks, each running off a separate drive. With the help of the Libraries' Systems Office, a menu was set up at the documents workstation for accessing a number of cartridges. At its peak, there were seven or eight cartridges at the workstation, each having six slots for holding CD-ROMs. The patron would then select the cartridge she wanted off the menu screen at the workstation, aided by an updated printed list containing the titles on each cartridge. The advantage of this system of access was that the patron did not have to touch the disks, but only to place a cartridge in the multi-disk changer and select an item off the menu.

In addition to processing and setting up the CD-ROMs at a workstation, some preliminary work had to be done with the disks prior to making them available at a public terminal. The liaison for United States government document CD-ROMs (Lou Vyhnanek) first had to see what type of information was contained on each disk or series of disks. In some cases, technical documentation came in the form of a separate pamphlet or volume with the CD-ROM. Often, however, the liaison had to access files directly on the disk, going to the DOS prompt or File Manager to see what material was contained on the disk and whether there were any instructions for using it. Usually, there was a README or documentation file that provided the information needed. Also, there were batch or execute files for running the disk at the terminal.

The main problem with all the different CD-ROMs published by the federal government was that there was no uniformity in the software used for running the disks.[1] The *1990 Census of Population, 1992 Economic Census*, and the *1992 Census of Agriculture* disks all run with GO software, which is menu-driven and can only search for one variable at a time, or with Extract, which is less user friendly but designed to search for multiple variables. However, other CD-ROMs developed by the Commerce Department, such as the *National Trade Data Bank,* and a wide variety of government agencies each have their own software for operating the disk. The liaison for United States government document CD-ROMs (Lou Vyhnanek) had to become familiar with these different types of software in order to develop instructions for the other Holland reference librarians and for the patrons using the CD-ROMs.

Initially, the agencies charged with producing the document CD-ROMs did not always provide enough information to assist the librarian setting up the disks. As a result, government documents librarians throughout the United States helped each other deal with the growing problem of providing access to these materials. The national government documents listserv, GOVDOC-L, became an excellent way to communicate and see how other librarians were coping with these resources. Documents librarians could subscribe to this listserv from a terminal in their offices and send messages for assistance when experiencing difficulties in dealing with a particular CD-ROM. Other librarians could reply, initiating a dialogue that often resolved problems before setting up the disk at the workstation.

Librarians also used GOVDOC-L to alert their colleagues about what was being done in their libraries to process these CD-ROMs. The Documents Librarian at Western Washington University (Robert Lopresti) developed a database of 1-2 page guides for using a number of document CD-ROMs called Docbase.[2] Others could use all or parts of this material to create their own set of instructions for individual CD-ROM titles. They could obtain Docbase material on disk or download it from the World Wide Web. This material has been very useful in developing the set of instructions currently used in Holland reference. Based on the short guides in Docbase, the liaison (Lou Vyhnanek), with the assistance of another Social Sciences Reference Librarian (Alison Manning), developed a set of short guides located at the government documents workstation.

Another way to begin to manage the large number of document CD-ROMs was to visit nearby libraries to learn what they were doing. At WSU, this involved visiting two librarians with responsibilities for documents CD-ROMs (Lily Wai and Bob Bolin) at the University of Idaho Library. One librarian (Bolin), in particular, was very helpful in sharing information he used to set up Idaho's CD-ROMs.

A final way of sharing information on the government CD-ROMs is to attend local workshops and Government Documents Roundtable sessions at the American Library Association national conferences. Representatives from the Depository Library Program speak at these sessions, which are a good way to find out about new developments. The Government Documents Roundtable also holds handout exchanges at the national conferences, which allow documents librarians to see what their colleagues are producing to show their patrons how to use the many different CD-ROMs.

MOVE TO THE NEW LIBRARY ADDITION

The situation for handling United States government documents CD-ROMs changed again with the move into the Holland/New Library building in May 1994. During this period, the liaison for United

States government document CD-ROMs (Lou Vyhnanek) was on sabbatical for a year and a Holland Humanities Reference Librarian (B. Jane Scales) absorbed these duties. During the move to the New Library building, the librarian made some changes in how things were set up at the documents workstation. All the government documents CD-ROM disks were taken out of the cartridges and placed in a large cabinet near the documents terminal by Superintendents of Documents call number. Using Auto Menu software, the librarian developed broad menu categories for grouping each of the individual titles, such as "Census of Population and Housing," for locating all the 1990 Census CD-ROMs. If a patron selected a title on the menu, a brief description of the contents of the disk would appear, along with the call number for the disk in the cabinet. Patrons would simply need to get the call number for the disk they wanted off the menu, retrieve it from the cabinet, put it in a caddy by the workstation, put the caddy into the CD-ROM drive, and select the item off the menu to run the disk.

With the Systems Office's assistance, batch files were set up to run the disk once it was inserted in the drive and return the patron to the main menu once she exited from the disk. Instructions at the new government documents workstation guided the patron in how to locate the needed disks and load them into the drive.

The move to the New Library building helped the librarians deal with an issue that had been around since the first United States government documents CD-ROM disks began to arrive: how to upgrade the Libraries' computer technology to provide needed access to these increasingly complex electronic products. Funds from the New Library building enabled the Libraries also to purchase needed equipment to provide more sophisticated access. When the new government documents workstation was set up in the New Library building, a more powerful 486 computer replaced the computer used in the old Holland building. The 486 helped run the growing number of CD-ROMs at this workstation, but more technology was needed again recently when the Systems Office added a higher speed CD-ROM drive to the configuration. It solved the problem of getting some of the government document CD-ROMs to work properly at the workstation. Technology will remain an issue, as the products produced require larger and more powerful machines to access the data. The Depository Library Program has also continually upgraded its "Minimum Technical Guidelines" for documents workstations and Holland reference needs to have terminals that conform to these standards.

About a year after the move into the New Library building, another problem arose in providing access to documents CD-ROMs. Some of the CD-ROM disks that the Libraries received contained raw data that required separate software such as Lotus, SAS, or SPSS to manipulate the numbers or other software that was not currently loaded on the government documents workstation in Holland reference. Some floppy disk material also needed separate spreadsheet or other software to access the material on the disk.[3] A place was needed in the Libraries where patrons could use this material or where they could check it out for use with the appropriate software on their own computers. To find a suitable location where these government documents CD-ROMs and floppy disks could be more readily made available, an ad hoc committee of three met and worked out an agreement to house some of the CD-ROMs and floppy disk materials in the Media Materials Services, where they could be used on-site or checked out.[4] In addition to United States government CD-ROMs and floppy disk materials, the agreement also covered data products from the Inter-university Consortium for Political and Social Research (ICPSR).

As a result of this agreement, liaisons from the Documents Processing Unit (Phyllis Ritter) and the Documents Serial Records Unit (Linda Crane) in the Technical Services Division were brought in so that these materials are now cataloged with the location "MMS." The agreement also provided that in the future, any documents CD-ROM requiring special software not available in Holland reference could be located in Media Materials Services. There are now well over 150 documents CD-ROM disks and floppy disks from both Holland and Owen (Sciences) housed in MMS.

In addition to moving some documents CD-ROMs requiring special software to Media Materials Services, a decision was also made to put some of the most heavily used CD-ROMs on the Holland's local area network (LAN). This meant that these disks would be located in towers run by servers in the Libraries' Systems Office and they could be accessed off the menus from a number of workstations in Holland reference, not just the government documents workstation. Currently the 1990 Census *Summary Tape File 3A* (Social and Economic Characteristics) disks for Washington and the United States, and the latest

Statistical Abstract of the United States, County and City Data Book, World Fact Book, and *National Criminal Justice Reference System (NCJRS)* disks are available through this local LAN. Two of these disks, *Statistical Abstract* and *NCJRS*, are available for access outside the library through software available on the Internet at the Systems Office's Home Page.

LATEST CHANGES

The latest changes in accessing government information involve greater reliance on electronic connections through databases such as GPO Access and STAT-USA, as well as locating material on the Internet through the World Wide Web. This does not mean that CD-ROM access will disappear, but that the federal government is giving electronic databases more emphasis. In late 1994 and early 1995, the government began to provide access to searching the full text of the *Federal Register, Congressional Record*, Congressional Bills, Public Laws, and other recent governmental information through an electronic database called GPO Access. At first, depository libraries were required to register with the government to use the system.

Libraries initially had a limited number of subscriptions to GPO Access either through a WAIS (Wide Area Information Server) or a SWAIS (Telnet) connection. At Washington State University Libraries, access was provided at first through a WAIS connection at workstations located at Holland, Owen, and the branch campus libraries. This was later changed to unlimited access through Netscape and the World Wide Web. Today, anyone who has an Internet address for GPO Access can connect to the database through Netscape or another graphical browser. At the Holland/New Library, GPO Access is available at several workstations, at "Quick Information" centers located throughout the New Library, and at the terminals at the Holland reference desk. Most recently, GPO Access has been added as a menu choice on Griffin, the Libraries' online catalog. Anyone with a Web browser such as Netscape can now access this database from outside the library.

Along with these changes in electronic access to government information, a Government Documents/Data Files Librarian (Joy Suh) came on board in August, 1996. This position would take charge of the Federal Depository Program for United States documents at

Washington State University Libraries and would take responsibility for documents in Holland reference. The librarian and the liaison for United States government document CD-ROMs (Lou Vyhnanek) worked out an arrangement to split the day-to-day responsibility for the documents CD-ROMs. To this end, the liaison has worked at familiarizing the new librarian with the setup at the government documents workstation, including the steps in the process of getting each CD-ROM ready for public use. This has worked out very well because in the past the liaison had often spent large amounts of time getting new CD-ROMs ready and available at the workstation. In particular, this involved learning how files were set up at the government documents workstation so new items could be added to the menu without calling on the Libraries' Systems Office for assistance. Often Systems' personnel were busy with other Libraries-wide problems and could not always immediately get to documents concerns. It also saved time for the liaison to be able to handle simple technical problems, with the major ones left for Systems to solve. Having two librarians working with new CD-ROMs has helped reduce the backlog of new titles and resulted in quicker availability of these disks at the workstation.

The new Government Documents/Data Files Librarian has also worked to provide other ways of accessing government information electronically. In addition to GPO Access, she has set up a single password access to STAT-USA, a government database that provides World Wide Web access to a wide range of current economic statistics, including all the material on the *National Trade Data Bank*. STAT-USA is available at a workstation in Holland reference set up with Ikiosk software, which allows users to search STAT-USA using Netscape but does not allow them to go to other locations on the World Wide Web. The librarian and the liaison have most recently set up a second Pentium government documents workstation for accessing government CD-ROMs that run in a Windows environment. This has been the most recent change in setting up the documents CD-ROMs. Many of the recent CD-ROMs require Windows software at the workstation in order to run the disk and Adobe Acrobat software for viewing PDF (Portable Document Format) files. These PDF files allow the user to print or download the exact image of the pages of a document. More and more government CD-ROMs contain material available only in PDF format. Holland reference now has a second workstation to access this material.

The amount of government agency information accessible through the Internet is also increasing rapidly. Through locations such as Fedworld, Federal Web Locator, and the University of Michigan's Documents Center Home Page, anyone with a computer capable of using a graphical browser such as Netscape can find a wealth of government information on the World Wide Web. Many depository libraries have developed their own home pages to provide links to key sites on the Internet. Future plans for the WSU Libraries' Home Page include a documents section to provide better access for its patrons to this everincreasing variety of information.

In conclusion, Holland reference at Washington State University Libraries has experienced and will continue to see widespread changes involving document CD-ROMs and electronic resources. The trend is clearly moving towards more information appearing in electronic format, particularly through connecting to it through the World Wide Web. Library catalogs are moving towards Web interfaces and government documents databases such as GPO Access fit well with this development. Access to federal information is becoming more complex, with more information available from a variety of sources. Librarians must be willing to change to meet this growing demand. They have to be able to develop the skills and have the necessary technology available to access information in these new formats. They also need to continue to increase their knowledge in order to help the user find their way through the growing amount of data available in electronic sources.

NOTES

1. Debora Cheney, "Technology in Documents Collections," *Management of Government Information Sources in Libraries,* ed. Diane H. Smith (Englewood, CO: Libraries Unlimited, 1993), 111-128; Susan M. Ryan, *Downloading Democracy: Government Information in an Electronic Age* (Cresskill, NJ: Hampton Press, 1996). Ryan's book has an excellent chapter titled, "Government Information on CD-ROM," 59-112.

2. Robert Lopresti, "Setting Up a Public Workstation with a Pioneer Six-Changer," *Government CD-ROMs: A Practical Guide to Searching Electronic Documents Databases*, ed. John Maxymuk (Westport, CT: Mecklermedia, 1994), 1-18. Maxymuk's book contains chapters written by documents librarians on specific government CD-ROMs. Other examples on what has been done at other libraries can be

found in Denise J. Johnson, "Processing, Storage, and Access to Government CD-ROM Publications in Depository Libraries," *Illinois Libraries* 75 (1993): 175-178.

3. Ryan, *Downloading Democracy,* 75-76, 113-131.

4. Members of the *ad hoc* committee were Siegfried Vogt, Head, Social Sciences Collection Development, Christy Zlatos, Head, Media Materials Services, and Lou Vyhnanek (then) Electronic Resource Librarian.

5. Ryan, *Downloading Democracy,* 176-196.

Embracing GIS Services in Libraries: The Washington State University Experience

Hyon-Sook (Joy) Suh
Angela Lee

SUMMARY. As a land-grant research university without a geography or cartography department, Washington State University Libraries present a unique organizational context for the adoption of GIS services. The authors consider the implementation of GIS services at the Washington State University Libraries, particularly at the Holland/New Library, which originated from an ARL/GIS Literacy Grant in 1992. The authors cover the following topics in the development of the service: Historical Background, System Architecture, Project Issues and Service Provision, Reference Services Policies, Current Implementation and Related Campus-Wide Issues, and Future Agenda. The services offered were essentially at a minimum level, that is, only providing limited access to government and commercial geospatial data using ArcView and Landview software. The approach to GIS in reference work has been to view it as a specialized service within a standard reference framework very similar to the computer-mediated searching programs of the past. Future plans for GIS services include shifting from a single desktop workstation to a system-wide network access to spatial data and maintaining a centralized repository for all spatial data whether purchased commercially or developed in-house. *[Article copies available for a fee from The Haworth Document Delivery Service: 1-800-342-9678. E-mail address: getinfo@haworthpressinc.com]*

Hyon-Sook (Joy) Suh is Government Documents/Data Files Librarian, Holland/New Library, Room 120M, Pullman, WA 99164-5610. Angela Lee is Head Librarian, School of Social Work Library, University of Washington, 252 Social Work/Speech and Hearing Building, Seattle, WA 98185.

[Haworth co-indexing entry note]: "Embracing GIS Services in Libraries: The Washington State University Experience." Suh, Hyon-Sook (Joy) and Angela Lee. Co-published simultaneously in *The Reference Librarian* (The Haworth Press, Inc.) No. 64, 1999, pp. 125-137; and: *Coming of Age in Reference Services: A Case History of the Washington State University Libraries* (ed: Christy Zlatos) The Haworth Press, Inc., 1999, pp. 125-137. Single or multiple copies of this article are available for a fee from The Haworth Document Delivery Service [1-800-342-9678, 9:00 a.m. - 5:00 p.m. (EST). E-mail address: getinfo@haworthpressinc.com].

125

For over the past ten years, many academic libraries have transformed their services by adding new technology. One transformation has been the adoption of GIS (Geographic Information Systems) technology in libraries. This article focuses on the evolution of GIS technology at Washington State University Libraries, particularly at the main Holland/New Library. As a land-grant research university without a geography or cartography department, Washington State University Libraries present a unique organizational context for the adoption of GIS services. The Libraries' primary clientele are faculty and students (1996 enrollment totals approx. 16,600 on the Pullman campus) where the surrounding area is a farming community, geographically isolated from a major metropolitan or industry-affiliated population.

The Libraries do not have a separate government documents department even though about 65 percent of all the items available through the Federal Depository Library Program are selected. The Holland/New Library, the humanities and social sciences library, houses a majority of the depository documents. The Owen Sciences and Engineering Library, the main science library, also houses a large portion of the depository collection including many maps while two smaller branch libraries, the Veterinary Medical/Pharmacy Library and the Brain Education Library, also house a few items. Given the Libraries' decentralized situation of handling documents and maps, efforts to integrate GIS services within the Libraries could be considered another unique example among libraries transforming with GIS technology.[1]

HISTORICAL BACKGROUND

The GIS program at Washington State University grew out of the initial project started by ARL in collaboration with the Environmental Systems Research Institute (ESRI) in 1992. The goal of the ARL/GIS Literacy Project was to provide a forum for research libraries to introduce, experiment with, and engage in GIS activities.[2] Each participating institution would receive free mapping software and training from ESRI in return for acting as a beta site for testing products, managing data, and sharing knowledge and experience related to GIS developments. The Director of Libraries (Nancy Baker) and the then Acting Head of the Humanities and Social Sciences Libraries (Mary

Gilles) decided to join the project with the idea that there would be potential demand for GIS around campus. The cost of providing GIS would be much higher if they waited to add the service without participating in the project.

For the initial project, participating institutions sent representatives to ESRI to review the overall ARL/GIS project and to receive initial training. The Assistant Director for Library Automation (John Webb) served as the initial contact and trainee for this Phase II of the project in Fall 1992. Then, the overall development of the project was passed on to a Holland Library Social Sciences Reference Librarian (Ralph Lowenthal), who had a background in library automation systems and an interest in this emerging technology, until he left the Libraries. At this time, the project was suspended temporarily because of technical and personnel issues. It was finally given to another Social Sciences Reference Librarian (Angela Lee), who was the subject specialist in Environmental Science and Geography, for full implementation.

In Fall 1994, the environmental science and geography subject specialist took on the task of developing and implementing the GIS program. The task was partially completed in several stages. First, the librarian sought background knowledge and training by enrolling in a course on the fundamentals of GIS and then by attending an ESRI ArcView training seminar in January 1995 with support from a Washington State Library grant. The next stage involved managing the equipment, software, and data necessary to run a GIS. Stage three was given to the development of a reference service policy, the writing of documentation, and the creation of instructional modules for librarians and users alike. The final step was to acquire funding for additional resources and to establish contacts with interested parties around campus. After setting up the system architecture, developing a reference service policy, and producing system documentation, the environmental science and geography subject specialist left the Libraries for another position in December 1995.

Although most of the details of the GIS program had been firmly worked out by this time, more remained to be accomplished. The Director of Libraries and the Head of Holland Public Services eventually adapted a Holland reference librarian position into a new, Government Documents/Data Files Librarian, who, among other duties, would take on the task of further developing and coordinating the GIS program.

In Fall 1996, the Government Documents/Data Files Librarian (Joy Suh), who had experience with GIS technology, began work at Holland Library. This led to new directions into the development and implementation of the program. The new librarian started developing a network of GIS interest groups around campus and an interdepartmental GIS team within the whole of the Libraries called the Data Sets Committee. The mission of the interdepartmental Data Sets Committee would be to define the Libraries' role and future plans.

SYSTEM ARCHITECTURE

GIS is an information system that requires functional capabilities for storing, accessing, and manipulating spatial data either in a manual or an automated enviroment.[3] In an automated environment, GIS is a tool that one can use to store spatial data for geographic features (roads, rivers, area boundaries, etc.) and associated data (population, environmental data, etc.) related to those features, retrieve and manipulate this data, and generate maps and statistics within a computer system. In other words, an automated GIS requires adequate hardware, software (database management and mapping), data elements, and personnel to support the system.

The necessary equipment and software to operate the system had already been purchased early on in the project. Equipment purchased at the time was relatively high-end; an 80486Dx2/33 mhz processor Gateway 2000 machine with 16 MB RAM, 1.3 GB hard drive, a 4X cd-rom drive, and a 15″ color monitor. ArcView software and spatial data (ArcUSA, ArcWorld, and Digital Chart of the World) were provided through the ARL/GIS Literary Project from ESRI. In addition, government data files such as Tiger/Line files and Landview mapping software, coupled with a commercial spatial data product (Wessex Tiger/Line 1992/1994) and 1990 Census STF1A and 3A (Wessex ProFiler) and database management systems software (Access and Dbase) were purchased as part of the project.

In developing any library GIS program one has to consider the design of the computer system for accessing the spatial information that will be offered. Both the actual design of the system and how that system is to be presented to the public are essential design features and comprise a critical part of the program development.

Two design decisions had to be addressed: how the front-end interface (data, software program icons) would look to the public and how the back-end load (drive/file management) would be organized. The system architecture had to meet several conditions that included: (1) logical placement of the data into categories for access and retrieval; (2) categories that were easily understood by librarians and technicians alike; (3) sufficient storage capacity allotted for the different GIS elements (spatial data, geo-referenced associated data, and software); (4) sufficient workspace for the user; and (5) space for temporary and permanent storage of software and data.

The first consideration for designing the back-end load was how to store the various types of software and government and commercial data products logically and flexibly on the hard drive.

The various products to be loaded on the drives were: mapping software (ArcView and Landview), the databases for spatial data (Wessex Tiger 92/94, ArcUSA, ArcWorld, DCW), the census demographic data set (Wessex ProFiler), and the database management systems (Access, Dbase). An efficient arrangement of these four kinds of products in the file management structure has critical access implications in terms of handling and linking the various kinds of data sets with the software.

The file management scheme for the hard drive setup was as follows:

1. The C-drive was loaded with the mapping software (ArcView and Landview), databases for spatial data (ArcUSA, ArcWorld, DCW), database management software (Access and Dbase), and temporary working directories for the workspace.
2. The D-drive held all the boundaries and associated census data provided by the commercial company (Wessex Tiger/92 and ProFiler). It was further divided into directories and subdirectories: USA, USCOUNTY, USSTATE. Washington state and county boundaries were loaded as a subdirectory of USCOUNTY and USSTATE to serve Washington-based clientele.
3. The E-drive was designed as the CD-ROM drive for reading data received or purchased on CD.

On the front-end interface, program icons were created in Windows-PC to facilitate easier access to data and software. The program icons were setup to reflect the pattern on the back-end load. Similar products and software were grouped together under one icon to appear together when one clicked on its icon. For example, the ESRI products such as ArcUSA (data), ArcWorld (data) and DCW (data) would all be categorized together. This allowed for easier manipulation of data and software, and was a general practice applied to the configuration of all GIS products.

PROJECT ISSUES AND SERVICE PROVISION

Like any project, setting up a GIS program at Washington State University Libraries posed several problems and questions. General concerns included a discussion of the role of the Libraries in providing GIS services, the users' needs, and the services that the Libraries should provide. The questions asked fell into five categories including service, personnel, technical, financial, and coordination issues. While some of these issues are specific to WSU Libraries, many could be applied to other libraries interested in setting up a GIS program. Below are some of the questions posed during project development. Also included is a description of how WSU Libraries approached those issues in the services that were to be provided.

Services: What services should be provided (full or partial GIS, reference or consultation, instruction or demonstration, production or self-service)? What should be the level of the services? Who should provide the services (librarians or technicians)? Who should use the services? Where should the GIS workstations be located (public workstations or computer lab office)? How should security be handled? Should the services be advertised? And, how?

Personnel: Who should provide the services? What is the librarian's role? Will technical staff install monitor and maintain the system? Who will manage the system?

Technical: Will there be technical assistance? What kind of format should be used? What kind of equipment and software is required? Where should data be stored? What kind of documentation should there be? And, should it be purchased or developed? What kind of security system is needed? What level of access do users get?

Financial: Can the institution afford full-time staff? Is there a budget for equipment, software, data, and grades? Are training funds available? Is there a specific budget for collections and services? Which disciplines/departments should pay for the services?

Coordination: What are the needs of the University campus? What GIS services are already available on campus? Which departments or disciplines might be interested in supporting such a service? What is the role of the library is providing services? Should the library coordinate GIS services across the campus or act as a resource contact?

The WSU Libraries' approach to these issues, given limited time and resources, was a simple one: to provide a scaled-down version of GIS in a one-person-acting-as-a-consultant mode. This scaled-down version of GIS was designed to be a specialized service within a standard reference framework very similar to the computer-mediated searching programs of the past. The rationale behind the services took into consideration the nature of the information (geospatial) and the considerable expertise required in order to handle such information. In a busy reference environment like Holland/New Library, providing complicated GIS services in a general public area did not seem wise or appropriate, given the kind of service it was, the in-depth assistance it required, and the limited knowledge and skills that the reference librarians had about the system.

Thus, the services offered were essentially at a minimum level, that is only providing access to government and commercial geospatial data and the use of ArcView and Landview software. Only one librarian, acting as part-time reference librarian and part-time GIS specialist, provided service assistance. The Libraries' Systems Office provided technical hardware and software support as needed. The librarian worked with users on a consultation basis only. Users were required to have some basic knowledge of GIS and to work with the librarian in planning their projects. The GIS workstation was placed in a locked computer room next to the librarians' offices, which was accessible to the public only by appointment. The room served as a place for the librarian to work on the GIS terminal and for office consultations on GIS projects. The room also provided security for equipment and

software and was a storage space for data, manuals, and other periph-
eral items.

System documentation was produced to log and monitor the project, to serve as a manual for other librarians, and to be included in
future tutorials and training manuals. Two introductory presentations
were given to reference librarians to demonstrate the system capabilities in late 1995. The librarians showed great interest in the system and
could see its obvious potential, but they also recognized the difficulties
ahead both in learning the system and in the need for funding support.
Because no budget was ever established for the GIS program, funding
was always limited. Requests for resources often had to be made to the
Director of Libraries (Nancy Baker) or the Assistant Director for
Library Automation (John Webb) at their discretion.

To aid in the coordination of GIS services among Washington State
University's departments and schools, a list of interested faculty and
staff was compiled for future reference and service planning.

REFERENCE SERVICE POLICIES

What are the implications for reference services and reference service policies? Because of the complexity in understanding and building a GIS program for the WSU Libraries, a whole new philosophy
had to be considered in offering services, developing user policies, and
defining the librarian's role. Several factors dictated a new approach to
reference policies including: (1) GIS services demand in-depth assistance not possible at a regular reference desk; (2) librarians have to
achieve a certain level of knowledge and skill to provide assistance;
and, (3) the use of specialized software and equipment is required for
dealing with questions. Below, under the categories of access services,
GIS user policies, librarian's role, and future planning, are some general policies and principles adopted in the WSU Libraries and some
recommendations for future planning:

> *Access Services:* (1) GIS services are specialized and offered on
> an appointment-only basis; (2) the Libraries will provide the
> basic equipment, software, and data sets; (3) the Libraries' will
> provide some basic instruction on the use of mapping software
> and some technical advice.

GIS User Policies: (1) users should have a basic knowledge of GIS or desktop mapping systems; (2) users should consult with the librarian to discuss a project prior to using the GIS software; (3) users must do their own work because the librarian provides only limited assistance; (4) users should bring their own supplies because facilities for saving users' work are not provided.

Librarian's Role: (1) librarians should have some basic knowledge of GIS to maintain their technical skills; (2) librarians should assist users on projects by providing data, giving hands-on training and technical assistance; (3) librarians should acquire and maintain new equipment, software, and data sets as deemed necessary; (4) librarians should know about national, regional, and local resources; and, (5) librarians should promote GIS literacy throughout the Washington State University Libraries and campus.

Recommendations for Future Planning: (1) a specialist librarian should be designated for GIS and he/she should receive continuous training to update skills; (2) the Libraries should serve as a repository for spatial data and software, made available for circulation, if needed by the department or agency; (3) a fund account should be created to purchase essential data sets in different disciplines; and, (4) a GIS interest group should be created to deal with service and acquisition issues.

CURRENT IMPLEMENTATION AND RELATED CAMPUS-WIDE ISSUES

The overall design of the GIS services and resultant policies at WSU Libraries provide an adequate response to the needs of the WSU community given the conditions that full-time staffing for GIS services is not extant and requests for this service are not frequent. As has been noted before, requests for the services are very labor intensive, requiring extensive assistance and monitoring during the user's interaction with the system.

Nevertheless, the Libraries' face several challenging issues. Most GIS users on campus are graduate students and faculty in Environmental Science, Agricultural Economics, or Forest, Soil, and Field

Diseases who have had their own access to GIS through their own laboratory facilities. Since 1990, these users have also had access to the Unix ArcInfo through the Digital Image Analysis Lab (DIAS) in the University's Information Technology Department. These so-called traditional users want data, particularly commercial GIS data, rather than analytical capability or mapping from the Libraries' facilities. In keeping, the Libraries' goal would be to function as a data repository for them. However, given the situation that the Libraries does not have a separate fund account for GIS and that the overall Libraries' budget is shrinking, increasing the support for GIS could create problems. First, when a requested GIS data set is considered to be interdisciplinary and the Libraries' fund accounting is by subject, who pays for the item? Second, acquiring commercial GIS data sets and software is often expensive and amounts to purchasing commitment over time like a serial. Budgetary support and disciplinary responsibility for GIS are still issues that need to be addressed at WSU Libraries. Providing a separate fund account for GIS would be a necessary first step in providing these services to our users.

A Data Sets Committee has been recently created to discuss these issues and to develop clearer policies and plans for GIS services.[4] The members of the Committee are five librarians from across WSU Libraries with GIS interests. Current Committee discussion topics include identifying basic commercial data sets that are needed for the teaching and research, developing a GIS collection development policy, developing strategies for getting funds for GIS data sets from inside and outside the Libraries, and planning for future GIS services. Future plans for GIS services include establishing an in-house data-repository of spatially referenced data sets and making the data sets available for system-wide access through the campus network and the internet. The Committee is currently contacting interested departments on campus to identify their GIS needs and expectations for the Libraries and seeking a way to develop a partnership for sharing existing departmental data sets through the Libraries' in-house data-repository.

At the same time, one way to guide patrons towards access to spatial data sets in the public domain is by constructing a GIS reference section within our existing library home page. Included on the home page would be GIS resources and data available for free on the internet. Web sites from government agencies such as the Census Bureau, the U.S. Geological Survey, and the EPA have spatial data and

Tiger files that can be downloaded by FTP. Other sources of resources and data are from various university GIS centers that provide state and local data with new, innovative approaches. The Map and Geographic Information Center at the University of Connecticut provides users with direct access to locally owned spatial data for downloading.[5] The Massachusetts Electronic Atlas Center at Harvard University helps users create their own maps through the internet by using various local socio-economic and health data in Massachusetts.[6] The ongoing project of the Alexandria Digital Library at the University of California at Santa Barbara, which is one of the six NSF-funded Digital Library Projects also provides digital spatial information including maps, satellite imagery, digitized photography, and associated metadata for all its holdings on the internet. Identifying, organizing, and accessing these useful web resources through the WSU Libraries' home page is another ongoing project.

Another environmental factor concerning the GIS community on the WSU campus is the lack of an appropriate coordinating agency for data sharing and facilitating communication among GIS users who are loosely organized into the GIS interest groups. Thinking that the Libraries could provide a better coordinating role, in Fall 1996 the Government Documents/Data Files Librarian created a listserv, WSUGIS-L (wsugis-l@listproc.wsu.edu). Since then, the librarian has identified many user needs and expectations in terms of acquiring GIS data sets and software through the listserv.

In order to manage the questions and concerns on the in-house listserv, WSUGIS-L, the librarian turns to various nationwide listservs to learn more about GIS. In addition to the already well-known listservs, GIS-L, MAPS-L, and ARLGIS-L, two new listservs developed in 1996 may be added to this list. GISTRANS-L is a useful source for sharing information about different file formats and ways of translating them from one format to another.[7] This listserv is especially useful where data in one format can or cannot be successfully translated into another format, which is a key element for GIS data acquisition and data storage activities. GISLIG-L is another list that discusses issues in providing GIS technology to libraries in general.[8] These lists provide not only a communication tool but also contain up-to-date knowledge for librarians in general.

FUTURE AGENDA

At Washington State University Libraries future plans for GIS services entail moving the GIS from a single desktop workstation towards providing system-wide access to spatial data. The role of the Libraries, then, would become one of maintaining a centralized repository for all spatial data whether purchased from a commercial vendor or developed in-house. System-wide access to a centralized repository requires additional hardware with a large storage capacity and networking capability. It also requires data maintenance, describing in-house spatial data in the MARC format based on the Content Standard Digital Geospatial Metadata[9] and the possible development of interactive protocol for the distribution of spatial data through the internet. These plans also require a substantial amount of human expertise to work out the details.

Continued promotion of GIS literacy around campus is essential to any future plans. This involves instruction in the basic concepts of GIS, software use, and the creation of a single map for non-traditional users. To promote a better understanding among librarians and staff, it also involves instruction in the content of databases and metadata including the spatial data transfer standard. Developing a series of GIS instructional programs and delivering them effectively within an appropriate time period again demand a full commitment of a librarian's time.

As one can read, the Washington State University Libraries experiment with GIS is a positive example of small-scale management of a large technical project. Since the Libraries started the GIS program from the ARL/GIS Literacy Project, efforts to develop and implement GIS services have been passed down from one Holland reference librarian to another with part-time responsibility for GIS. With the limited resources described, the Libraries' role has been transformed from simply providing basic spatial data (Tiger/Line files, for example) to consulting, giving basic instruction using GIS technology, and helping users capture spatial data from the internet. For systematic implementation and planning for GIS services at WSU Libraries, the recent answer has been the development of the Data Sets Committee. The future success of the GIS program depends on how this Committee aggressively works with funding and how the Libraries' administration supports basic needs, including personnel and up-to-date equipment necessary for implementing these future plans for GIS services.

NOTES

1. Patrick McGlamery and Melissa Lamont. "Geographic Information Systems in Libraries: New Opportunities and Challenges," *DATABASE* 17 (December 1994): 35-44. To find other examples, see also the *Journal of Academic Librarianship* 21(July 1995) and *Information Technology and Libraries* 14 (June 1995). The two issues devoted the whole volume to the topic on GIS and libraries.

2. Nancy M. Cline and Prudence S. Alder. "GIS and Research Libraries: One Perspective," *Information Technology and Libraries* 14 (June 1995):111.

3. Jeffrey Star and John Estes. Geographic Information Systems (Englewood Cliffs, NJ: Prentice-Hall Inc. 1990): P. 3.

4. The current members of the Data Sets Committee include five librarians: Adonna Fleming from the Owen Sciences and Engineering Library; Joy Suh, Government Documents/Data Files Librarian; Siegfried Vogt, Head of the Social Science Collection Development; John Webb, Assistant Director for Library Automation; and Christy Zlatos, Head of the Media Material Services.

5. MAGIC can be reached at http://magic.lib.uconn.edu.

6. Massachusetts Electronic Atlas can be reached at http://icg.harvard.edu/~mpas/maatlas.htm.

7. GISTRANS-L (subscription address: Majordomo@avenza.com).

8. GISIG-L (subscription address: Majordomo@virginia.EDU).

9. For an updated version, access to http://www.fgdc.gov/Metadata/metahome. html. Also, the relationship between the Content Standard Digital Geospatial Meta-Data and the US MARC format can be found in the article by Elizabeth U. Mangan, "The Making of a Standard," *Information Technology and Libraries* 14 (June 1995): 99-110.

Appendix 1:
About Washington State University Libraries' Holland Reference Services

Christy Zlatos

SUMMARY. Holland Reference Services, the largest reference unit of Washington State University Libraries, dates from the merger of two divisional libraries, the Humanities Library and the Social Sciences Library in 1978. In this appendix, the author presents some of Holland's history and vital statistics. *[Article copies available for a fee from The Haworth Document Delivery Service: 1-800-342-9678. E-mail address: getinfo@haworth pressinc.com]*

When your guest editor arrived in Pullman for her interview for an advertised Social Sciences Reference Librarian position in 1991, Holland Library (the structure completed in 1951) was full to the gills and the Holland Addition (as it was then called) was an enormous hole directly beside Holland Library. The car pulled up next to the hole, headlights on (because it was night), and everyone got out (though it was raining cats and dogs) to inspect the digging. That the structure planned for the hole with its large, central atrium and piano shape was

Christy Zlatos is Head, Media Materials Services, Holland/New Library, Room 1-C, Washington State University Libraries, Pullman, WA 99164-5610 (E-mail: ZLATOS@MAIL.WSU.EDU).

[Haworth co-indexing entry note]: "Appendix 1: About Washington State University Libraries' Holland Reference Services." Zlatos, Christy. Co-published simultaneously in *The Reference Librarian* (The Haworth Press, Inc.) No. 64, 1999, pp. 139-147; and: *Coming of Age in Reference Services: A Case History of the Washington State University Libraries* (ed: Christy Zlatos) The Haworth Press, Inc., 1999, pp. 139-147. Single or multiple copies of this article are available for a fee from The Haworth Document Delivery Service [1-800-342-9678, 9:00 a.m. - 5:00 p.m. (EST). E-mail address: getinfo@haworthpressinc. com].

antithetical to the strict, modular "functionalism" of the old Holland building with its 9-foot ceilings was not apparent to the casual observer. The view was actually a study of taste in library buildings over the last 50 years.

The largest reference unit of the Washington State University Libraries, Holland Reference Services may be defined as the traditional name given the humanities/social sciences/ (and possibly) undergraduate reference service that used to be based in the original structure, the E. O. Holland Library. Holland Reference defined as just the humanities and social sciences dates from 1977 when the sciences moved down the hill to their completed Owen Science and Engineering Library. In 1978, the Humanities and the Social Sciences divisional libraries combined to make a joint operation. When a 34 million-dollar addition was completed in 1994, called simply New Library, Holland reference moved to some new, swanky digs there. Today, the Humanities and Social Sciences collections are housed in the combination of Old Holland and the New Library, called Holland/New Library, and the Holland Reference Services continues to call itself Holland while providing most of its service (except for microforms) from the addition.

Also called the Hum/Soc reference staff dating from 1978 when Hum joined Soc (or vice versa, depending on whether you hailed from Hum or Soc), the Holland reference staff presently numbers 12. Each week during Fall and Spring Semester, 87.25 hours are staffed by professional librarians and information assistants at the reference desk. Professional librarians typically work double-staffed, and, since Fall 1995, they have been assisted by paraprofessional information assistants. Two types of information assistants are utilized on the Holland reference desk: full-time classified staff employees who work alongside the librarians during the business day and graduate students who also work alongside librarians but also cover the night hours alone from 10:00 until 11:45 PM. Although working alongside information assistants was considered initially a revolutionary endeavor, for the most part, Holland librarians regard the information assistant experiment as very successful.

An average daytime desk shift for a Holland reference librarian is 2.5 hours. Combined with one night shift per week and approximately 6 weekend shifts per semester, a professional librarian's desk workload is approximately 14 hours per week.

But, perhaps this is changing. An audit of Holland reference librarians workload took place during the Summer of 1997; 5 factors were considered in the workload mix in order to promote equitable workloads. These factors were professional and scholarly activities/ service (calculated as up to 20% for each librarian), collection development/departmental liaison, unit coordination/employee supervision, user education, electronic resources, and reference. Whereby the old method was to keep everybody's number of reference shifts as equal as possible, the new method offered librarians heavily involved in other worthwhile pursuits less reference shifts.

Traditionally, the duties of Holland librarians have been three-fold: reference, collection development, and user education. These were considered much like a stool; each of the three was needed in equal amounts to sit upright as a professional librarian. That professional and scholarly activities/service, coordination/supervision, and electronic resources figured equally into the audit is an acknowledgement of these activities in the workload (including selecting and maintaining those gazillion electronic resources). The workload audit is considered another revolutionary experiment.

When asked if the new audit is working, answers were mixed and the jury is still out. Some Holland reference librarians thought some of their duties were so esoteric that they escaped the audit. Others thought that the audit had marvelously acknowledged their participation (for once). Some that speculated that if the Director of Libraries as Interim Head, hadn't initiated the project, the workload audit could have never been achieved.

As noted above, Holland's reference tradition is rooted in the ideal of the departmental library where librarians considered patron inquiries and needs from a pure disciplinary standpoint. The three legs of the traditional stool noted above have enabled Hum/Soc reference librarians to offer great in-depth research assistance. This traditional stool is changing. Modern realities such as expanding enrollment, dwindling budgets, exploding technology, and distance education all demand consideration. Holland reference librarians must continue to adapt and augment their services in order to continue to best serve their clientele.

THE HOLLAND REFERENCE SERVICE

The question of what characterizes or distinguishes Holland from all others stumped many Holland reference librarians. When asked, many said to write about demographics. The main campus of Washington State University at Pullman is a rural campus; most Holland reference customers come from the 16,000 undergraduates and 2,000 graduates who comprise the student body. Although WSU students come from the 50 states and 90 countries (there are 1,500 international students), over 80 percent come from the state of Washington. Holland reference librarians meet 19-year-olds in droves every workday.

Most librarians would agree that it is the combined expertise and camaraderie of its membership that makes the reference service special. Holland librarians are hired for their subject expertise in order to complement the whole. Considered either Hum or Soc upon hire, reference librarians offer specialized reference services, user education, and collection development liaison work with the academic departments in their subject disciplines. Although traditionally only a very few librarians cross the line from Hum into Soc (or vice versa) and develop the collections in both areas, in recent times more librarians are crossing the line and working in both camps. Believing that reference service is the most important ingredient for success, in recent years, Holland librarians have resisted colleagues offering to do collection development in a subject area or two without the requisite reference desk duty. Holland librarians also believe their reference service is made stronger by their strong commitment to user education.

Whenever a vacancy occurs, everyone in the department discusses the departing colleague's subject specialties and collection development workload, whether Soc or Hum, in a departmental staff meeting and the subject specialties are divvied up or considered for trade. Working in new and different subject areas is considered a great way to pump up a tired career, or an antidote for boredom. The position that ends up advertised in the trade magazines is a position thought to complement the new whole. It is the result of a consensus decision.

FACULTY STATUS

Holland reference librarians have been members of the Washington State University faculty officially since 1946. As members of the faculty, this means professional librarians are responsible for the requisite national participation, service, and publication. Librarians are ranked in grades 2, 3, or 4 and these rankings are equivalent to the academic ranks of assistant professor, associate professor, and professor.

Although librarians have debated the notion of being faculty versus not being faculty over the years, Holland librarians take their faculty status seriously. Because it is often very difficult to fit research and writing into a regular workweek, WSU librarians qualify each week for four hours of Professional Activity Time (PAT). Sabbaticals are also available for tenured faculty and are factored either as half-year at full salary or full-year at three-quarters-salary. Recent sabbatical projects of Holland reference librarians include print publications such as *The Directory of Music Resources in the Pacific Northwest* (Pacific Northwest Chapter, Music Library Association), *Children and Adjustment to Divorce: An Annotated Bibliography* (Garland Press), *Unorganized Crime: Criminal Activity in New Orleans during the 1920's* (in progress, Center for Louisiana Studies, University of Southwestern Louisiana), and web-based productions such as Ecoventure URL <http:// 134.121.164.23/ecoventure.htm> and the Holland Library Data Archive (HLDA) <http:// www.mms.edu/mms/documents/hlda/hlda.html>.

Many colleagues remember stronger library faculties of the past when librarians stood together around their Library Faculty Affairs Committee (LFAC) to fight intrusion and institutional craziness. Such was the incident in 1975 when a WSU instructional faculty member and folklorist didn't get tenure in English but told colleagues at a cocktail party not to worry because he would be coming to work in the Libraries soon. The rumor checked out and the library faculty was outraged. But, after rallying around LFAC, the library faculty explained the importance of the accredited MLS to the then Vice President–Academic who abandoned the pursuit.

In comparison, today's library faculty is rather soft.

AN INTERNATIONAL AWARENESS

Librarians at Washington State University Libraries have always maintained a strong interest in international librarianship. They have demonstrated this awareness by their participation in international library associations including IFLA, by gathering and sending books abroad to universities in China, the Soviet Union, and to our sister university at Far Eastern State in Vladivostok, and by participating in international exchanges including Fulbrights.

Collectively, either as sabbaticals or in other releases from full-time employment, Holland reference librarians have traveled all over to parlay their library skills and deliver papers in the countries of the world. This experience comes in handy every day in working at the reference desk with both the 1,500 international students at WSU as well as rest of the graduate and undergraduate student body.

GOVERNANCE

For whatever reason–some say the heads need tenure when they arrive *en scene,* some say it is just impossible to bring one in from outside–it is very difficult to keep a Head, Holland Public Services in the position. Since the 70's, Holland has had just short of a half dozen heads and acting heads. During the Director of Libraries' recent tenure as Interim Head, Holland librarians, in a move that dovetailed with a greater reorganization process occurring within the whole of Washington State University Libraries, decided to remake the position in the form of a departmental chair. Tenured Holland librarians could be elected to serve for a renewable three-year term. At the present time, Holland librarians, at a loss as to what to title the position (the Library Director is both the dean and chair of the Libraries), still refer to the position as Head. During the summer 1997, the first elected Head was chosen.

Although the Holland reference librarians function as faculty members and as equals, three coordinating positions traditionally have been associated with Holland Reference Services: a Head of Reference, a Head, Humanities Collection Development, and a Head, Social Sciences Collection Development. These positions have evolved since the 70s.

The Holland, Head of Reference is responsible for reference scheduling and also manages a classified staff employee who does materials processing and students who do shelving as well as the information assistants noted above. Before the last budget cuts, this Head managed a staff of three full-time classified staff who also did pre-order searching and preparation for collection development. Three classified staff positions were cut to one when it was decided that pre-order searching duplicated work occurring in technical services, a luxury Holland librarians would have to live without.

During the Fall semester 1997, a new Head of Reference was promoted into the position from the unit when the previous one stepped

down during the previous July to pursue other interests in the department. Whereas the old Head is nationally recognized for exploring
training issues in librarianship and had instituted an intensive 4-week
training program for all new hires, it is unknown whether the new
Head will maintain the program or create something entirely new.

The two Heads, Collection Development coordinate both halves,
Soc and Hum (or vice versa) of the Holland library materials budgets.
Always quick to remind colleagues that the Humanities and Social
Sciences materials budgets never merged in 1978 but have always
remained separate, collection development is administered by each of
these Heads in a little different manner. However, both Heads have
coordinated collection development through both good times and bad;
the last big Libraries-wide serials cancellation occurred in 1994. During Summer 1997 after the old Head retired, a new Head, Humanities
Collection Development was selected also from within the unit. Just
what changes this new Head will bring remains to be seen.

USER EDUCATION

As conceived by a director years ago, the User Education Office
works to unify the disparate, departmental interests of Holland (Hum/
Soc) and the Owen (Science) Libraries by coordinating user education
Libraries-wide. The Office, consisting of two professional librarians, a
Head, User Education and an Assistant Head, stands apart from the
Holland Public Services administrative change in that the Head reports
directly to the Director of Libraries. While the Head, User Education
does reference shifts at the Holland reference desk, the Assistant Head
(pending a nationwide search that is underway) will do reference shifts
in the area library most suited by field. Coordinators for user education
exist presently in Holland, Owen, and the Veterinary Medical/Pharmacy
libraries; these librarians receive updates and exchange ideas by serving
on CLUE, the Committee for Libraries User Education.

Believing that reaching student hordes through teaching groups is
more dynamic than working one-at-a-time with patrons at the reference desk, librarians throughout the Libraries are strong proponents of
user education. Last year, the combined number of bibliographic instruction sessions and general orientation tours for the entire library
system numbered 235 groups reaching over 5,428 persons.

UNIVERSITY 300

Originally developed by librarians as a one-credit course in WSU's Extended Degree Program, University 300 directly addresses the need for instruction in using the Internet for research. What began as a course taught over the Internet with a coursebook and a sequence of 13 videotapes has gradually evolved into a completely web-based sequence of teaching modules that can be viewed at <http://www.wsulibs.wsu.edu/univ300/campus/univ300.htm>. The University 300 teaching modules have blossomed into a promising model for teaching library research throughout the WSU curriculum.

NEW TECHNOLOGICAL FRONTIERS

From the time that the first CD-ROM product, *Compact Disclosure,* was introduced in Holland reference in 1987, the many and various technological applications simply have exploded and changed the environment. These applications include but are not limited to database and CD-ROM management; web-based technology pursuits such as the Libraries' Home Page creation and maintenance, user education teaching module design, or web-based OPAC customization; and GIS (Geographic Information Systems) services. In order to manage and plan for technology, Holland librarians have responded in basically two ways: (1) they serve on Libraries-wide committees and task forces charged with management or problem solving, and (2) they have endowed four Holland reference positions with responsibilities as electronic resource librarians.

CONCLUSION

As Holland Reference Services is based on consensus and consideration, radical changes in response to a changing information landscape are difficult. The changes that have come have been gradual and, certainly talked about.

Perhaps the most radical change of all came late in 1997, when the Libraries bought the UMI product, ProQuest Direct, and installed it as a button on the web-based OPAC's gateway. Much of the contents of

ProQuest Direct is full-text and the mega-database has had an instant effect of noticeably reducing traffic at the Holland reference desk. Instead of greeting customers standing in line for initial guidance, librarians saw students either helping themselves at the public terminals or no longer even coming into the library. If the Holland librarians suspected their imaginations were at play, initial statistics from UMI confirmed all suspicions. From January to February 1998, Holland in-house building use increased from 7,000 to 21,000 searches; and, the use of the roaming ID outside the Libraries increased from 4,000 to 16,000 searches.

These statistics have caused some soul searching for Holland librarians who wonder if students are getting appropriate materials. Certainly students are becoming so skilled and using databases so simple that help with navigation is needed less and less although help with the interpretation of the information seems to be needed more and more.

Certainly the way that Holland librarians provide assistance will have to change in order to help remote users. In the short time Holland librarians have experienced ProQuest Direct, they have discovered that an initial approach of suggesting that telephone callers stop by for one of the carefully-prepared paper handouts needed to be scrapped in favor of providing web-based materials that could be made instantly available. Also, the web-based materials needed to be specifically prepared as the paper handout readily listed the log-on and password that needed to be protected from the off-campus remote users of the web.

The question was also raised about how will Holland librarians come to know the customers who use ProQuest Direct from remote sites. Certainly the only information initially available for these customers is on the UMI management reports.

Will ProQuest Direct or similar databases have a lasting effect on Holland Reference Services? Only time will tell.

Appendix 2:
A Chronology of the History
of Washington State University Libraries

Christy Zlatos

SUMMARY. Washington State University, located in Pullman at the southeastern edge of the state, has an enrollment of approximately 20,000 on its main campus and that of its three branches (Tri-Cities, Spokane, and Vancouver). This chronology of the history of the Washington State University Libraries offers readers a sense of our scale, something of our direction, and our interests. *[Article copies available for a fee from The Haworth Document Delivery Service: 1-800-342-9678. E-mail address: getinfo@haworthpressinc.com]*

1889 Washington is admitted to the Union.

1892 College opens as Washington Agricultural College, Experiment Station, and School of Science, a land-grant college.

1892 The first library opens as a shelf in the college President's office at the "Crib," the name students give the first campus building.

1893 The first Administration opens and the Library moves to a "convenient and well lighted room."

Christy Zlatos is Head, Media Materials Services, Holland/New Library, Room 1-C, Washington State University Libraries, Pullman, WA 99164-5610 (E-mail: zlatos@mail.wsu.edu).

[Haworth co-indexing entry note]: "Appendix 2: A Chronology of the History of Washington State University Libraries." Zlatos, Christy. Co-published simultaneously in *The Reference Librarian* (The Haworth Press, Inc.) No. 64, 1999, pp. 149-155; and: *Coming of Age in Reference Services: A Case History of the Washington State University Libraries* (ed: Christy Zlatos) The Haworth Press, Inc., 1999, pp. 149-155. Single or multiple copies of this article are available for a fee from The Haworth Document Delivery Service [1-800-342-9678, 9:00 a.m. - 5:00 p.m. (EST). E-mail address: getinfo@haworthpress.inc.com].

1893 The first librarian, Mrs. Nancy Van Doren (1893-99), is listed in the college catalog. In addition to being the librarian, Van Doren also serves as professor of English and preceptress of the dormitory for women.

1897 Miss Miriam Tannatt (1897-98), daughter of a member of the Board of Regents, serves as the first full-time librarian. This is during the school-year 1897-98.

1899 Miss Gertrude Saxton (1899-1908), a professional librarian who "graduated with good rank in the eighth training class [of the Los Angeles Public Library] in May 1897, is hired to head the Library. Saxton moves the Library from its room to better quarters in the attic of the Administration building, institutes the first accession record, and begins cataloging by typing cards with an early typewriter. In 1908, she resigns to marry a faculty member.

1909 Professionally trained at the New York State Library School under Dr. Melvil Dewey, Asa Don Dickinson (1909-12), a capable young librarian, is recruited. As the first librarian to work in the first constructed library building, a combination library/auditorium called Bryan Hall, Dickinson buys books, institutes rules and regulations, and establishes a bindery.

1912 Dickinson institutes the first course on "How to Use the Library."

1912 Albert Sherwood Wilson (1912-15) becomes Librarian, is first to criticize the College's practice of allocating funds to academic departments, and suffers an early death.

1915 W.W. Foote (1915-46) is appointed Librarian and serves until his retirement in 1946. Called the "Jesse James" of librarianship for his notable successes in trading duplicates with over 200 libraries, Foote accepts any gift, large or small, and counts all as gifts–even the stuff he plans to trade. Foote is known for old-fashion style of administering the Library with his restrictive policies, closed stacks, and dark, poorly ventilated reading rooms.

1937 Evergreen (student newspaper) editorial decries limited library services in the evenings. President Holland and Foote begin considering a new library building but plans are halted by World War II.

1938 Friends of the Library is established by President Holland.

1946 By the time Foote retires, general holdings skyrocket to 500,000. Post-war enrollment begins to explode.

1946 Wilson Compton (1946-51) becomes President of the College. He writes that the Library should gradually become the intellectual center of the Inland Empire.

1946 Compton establishes a "Committee of Forty" that determines the following list of criticism of the Library:

- It has too few trained librarians.
- Many serial collections are incomplete.
- Important seminal works are lacking in the collection.
- Insufficient funds are allotted to the purchase of important publications.
- It has an antiquated and time-consuming purchasing policy.
- Books and periodicals are not readily available because they are located in departmental libraries.

1946 G. Donald Smith (1946-76) becomes Librarian in November. He begins to cull the bulk of the many Foote collections as well as brighten the reading rooms.

1946 The Board of Regents decree, on April 11, that professional librarians shall become a constituent part of the College's faculty.

1947 Money comes through for a new library building and Smith scuttles the Foote plan for a new building in favor of the efficient, "modular" construction made popular by nationally-known library architect, Angus Snead McDonald.

1948 Construction begins.

1950 Smith decides to organize the library into 3 divisions for the Humanities, Social Sciences, and Natural and Physical Sciences. The staffs of the divisional libraries are to develop each discipline independently in the best way to serve the clientele.

1950 Named the Ernest O. Holland Library, the building is finished. Students gather in August to make a human chain from the old library, Bryan Hall, to Holland in order to move the books. When returning to campus old-time Cougar alumni still talk about it.

1951 The card catalog is moved from Bryan Hall and duplicated by the Remington Rand, Dexigraph method. The second copy of the catalog is separated for each of the three divisional libraries. The original remains in a Readers' Services Division.

1951 Compton resigns under mysterious circumstances that merit an article in *Life* (Magazine), titled "Picture of a Good Man Who Is Getting the Ax." *Life* 30 (June 11, 1951):49-50+.

1952 President C. Clement French (1952-67) replaces Compton.

1952 A color film slide series and the first guide to the Library, *The WSC Library Handbook* appear. A revised edition of the *Handbook* follows in 1953, and new editions in 1955, 1960, and 1962.

1954 The Audio-Visual Center, located in the Library basement, and previously a separate unit, becomes part of the Library.

1957 First Listening Laboratory opens in the Library.

1959 The College officially becomes Washington State University.

1959 Although the presence of the central Holland Library has extinguished a lot of the departmental book buying, two proposals for a divisional library for Engineering and Related Sciences and a departmental Chemistry Library are proposed. (Neither of these proposals materialized although the Owen Sciences and Engineering Library that met the demand for these libraries opened in 1977.)

1962 A Graphics Laboratory opens.

1963 The Library becomes a member of the Association of Research Libraries (ARL) in January.

1963 Two small departmental libraries (still in operation) an Education Library and a Veterinary Sciences Library, open.

1964 Smith holds a Total Library Staff Meeting to discuss automation. He tells everyone that the Library is ideally suited to become a leader in this new field.

1965 A proposal for an undergraduate library is presented and discussed on campus but never implemented.

1966 Smith creates the first Library Systems Division with a faculty position as Systems Analyst and several programmers.

1967 French resigns and W. Glenn Terrell (1967-85) becomes University President.

1968 Through an NSF grant, the first automated acquisitions system, LOLA (Library On-Line Acquisitions Sub-System), is developed.

1968 Listening Laboratory is updated with new equipment.

1968 The Senate Library Committee and the central management agree on a compromise concept regarding campus departmental libraries by which the departmental libraries will be integrated into such related units as a hoped-for Science Area Library.

1972 The Library joins forces with the Washington State Library to parlay the newly-developed acquisitions system with its capacity for fiscal reports into a component of the statewide system.

1973 The MRAP (ARL Management Review and Analysis Program) Study (1973-74) takes place at the Library.

1974 Due to financial difficulties of the Richard Abel Company, the Library's approval program is interrupted and a special effort is made to get the 1974-75 imprints.

1976 Longtime Director, G. Donald Smith retires and Allene Schnaitter (1976-82) is appointed on July 1.

1977 The statewide bibliographic system called Western Library Network (WLN) comes online.

1977-78 The Owen Sciences and Engineering Library opens and the Sciences Divisional Library moves out of the Holland Library. The Humanities Library and the Social Sciences Library merge in the Holland Library building and become Holland Public Services. The modern phase of the Washington State University Libraries begins.

1979 The card catalog is closed at WSU Libraries; a COM catalog is adopted.

1981 First major system-wide serial expenditure reduction is mandated.

1981 The Libraries first online catalog, developed in-house in conjunction with WLN, is brought up with a command system.

1984 The George W. Fischer Agricultural Sciences Branch Library is dedicated in the Johnson Hall Annex. First established in 1974-75, the original library was located in Johnson Hall.

1984 Allene Schnaitter resigns and Professor and longtime friend-of-the-Libraries, Don Bushaw agrees to serve as Interim Director.

1985 W. Glenn Terrell resigns and Samuel H. Smith (1985-present) becomes Washington State University President. His objectives are fourfold: a restructuring of the undergraduate curriculum to emphasize core courses; to establish branch campuses in Spokane, the Tri-Cities, and Vancouver (Campus libraries are eventually established in each area); to raise the stature of research and graduate work; and to implement a step-salary system to attain equity in salaries to support the faculty.

1985 Maureen Pastine (1985-89) becomes Library Director. She promotes national participation and research and writing for tenure.

1986 Cougalog becomes the name of the online catalog in a contest held during National Library Week.

1988 Head, User Education is hired (who would report to the Director) and a centralized User Education unit for the Libraries is established. User education is a special interest of Pastine's. Requests for instruction skyrocket.

1988 EZSEARCH, the WSU Libraries' user-friendly interface to its online catalog, the Cougalog, is introduced.

1988 The Architecture Library becomes a branch library in July.

1989 Funding comes for a Holland Library Addition and planning begins. Pastine resigns and Don Bushaw again agrees to serve as Interim Director. When he becomes ill, Associate Director, Donna McCool steps in and serves as Interim Director.

1991 Nancy L. Baker becomes Library Director.

1991 Funding comes from a major software developer, Software AG, to market some of our programming for our online catalog as Tapestry.

1992 Second major system-wide serials expenditure reduction is mandated.

1992 The online catalog's "Serials Control Module" is completed.

1994 As a cost-saving measure, OCLC is substituted for WLN as the Libraries' bibliographic utility.

1994 The Addition becomes known as the New Library. The entire staff participates in the Library Move; they get t-shirts and their picture taken. The New Library Dedication takes place on August 25, 1994.

1995 The Libraries purchase an Innovative Interfaces catalog as a joint library catalog with Eastern Washington University. It is named "Griffin" in honor of the mythical creature that is half Cougar-like (WSU mascot) and half Eagle-like (EWU mascot).

1996 The Libraries undergo a "planning process" in order to reorganize. A facilitator from the Association of Research Libraries is brought in to kick off the process and the Planning Committee creates a Mission, Values, and Vision Statement. A new organization (with chart) is produced.

1997 A Web version of Griffin comes up for users.

1997 The implementation of the new organization begins.

Appendix 3:
From the Siegfried A. Vogt Archive:
Selected Documents
and Memoranda from the '70s
in Honor of Pauline Lilje

Siegfried A. Vogt

SUMMARY. To better understand the roots of Holland Reference Services in two divisional libraries, the Humanities Library and the Social Sciences Library, the author has culled the Archive in honor of Pauline Lilje in order to show readers some of his favorite original documents from the '70s. *[Article copies available for a fee from The Haworth Document Delivery Service: 1-800-342-9678. E-mail address: getinfo@haworthpressinc. com]*

The following documents and memoranda from the Siegfried A. Vogt Archive are presented in order to illustrate the world of the divisional libraries in the 70s. Several have been written by Pauline Lilje and date from the time she was Chief of the Social Sciences Library (1974-8). The following documents are in chronological order, and need no further explanation.

Dr. Siegfried A. Vogt is Head, Social Sciences Collection Development, Holland/ New Library, Room 120D, Washington State University Libraries, Pullman, WA 99164-5610 (E-mail: vogt@wsu.edu).

[Haworth co-indexing entry note]: "Appendix 3: From the Siegfried A. Vogt Archive: Selected Documents and Memoranda from the '70s in Honor of Pauline Lilje." Vogt, Siegfried A.. Co-published simultaneously in *The Reference Librarian* (The Haworth Press, Inc.) No. 64, 1999, pp. 157-185; and: *Coming of Age in Reference Services: A Case History of the Washington State University Libraries* (ed: Christy Zlatos) The Haworth Press, Inc., 1999, pp. 157-185. Single or multiple copies of this article are available for a fee from The Haworth Document Delivery Service [1-800-342-9678, 9:00 a.m. - 5:00 p.m. (EST). E-mail address: getinfo@haworthpressinc.com].

157

As follows:

Document 1. Pauline Lilje, "S. Vogt: Areas of Responsibility Social Science Library, July, 1972." (Original has tape marks.)

Document 2. Pauline Lilje, "Reference Training Schedule: July 1-23" and "S. Vogt's Training Schedule 24 July-28 July." (1972)

Document 3. Pauline Lilje Memorandum to Social Science Librarians. May 27, 1974, "Information for Discussion at Tuesday Meeting, May 28th, 12:00, Rm 160B."

Document 4. Organization of the Social Sciences Division Library: 1976/1977.

Document 5. Pauline Lilje Memorandum to Director, G. Donald Smith. (four pages, dated May, 1976). G. Donald Smith's Reply (two pages, dated June 14, 1976). Includes Pauline Lilje's Cover Memorandum to the Staff. (February 1977)

Document 6. Allene Schnaitter, Director of Libraries to the Library Staff. Administrative Organization of the Library. (Six page plus organization chart, August 1977).

Document 7. Pauline Lilje Memorandum to Audrey Dibble. "Next Semester's Reference Schedule." (January, 1978)

Document 8. Pauline Lilje Memorandum to Ron, Force, Assistant Director of Public Services. "Job Responsibilities." (September 17, 1979)

DOCUMENT 1. Pauline Lilje, "S. Vogt: Areas of Responsibility So-cial Science Library, July, 1972." (Original has tape marks.)

S. Vogt: Areas of Responsibility
Social Science Library, July, 1972

AREA	SUPERVISOR	APPROXIMATE PERCENT
Reference	Pauline Lilje	25 to 35
Revision		
1. New Books	Adrien Taylor	
	Pauline Lilje	15-6
2. Social Science Shelf List	Pauline Lilje	
3. Some Author/Title Card Catalog	Pauline Lilje	10-4
Collection Maintenance	Adrien Taylor	15-6
Micro Filing (HRAF, UN, US, etc.)	P. Lilje will route you to the appropriate supervisor	5-2
Serial Record	Warren Babcock	20-8

DOCUMENT 2. Pauline Lilje, "Reference Training Schedule: July 1-23" and "S. Vogt's Training Schedule 24 July-28 July." (1972)

REFERENCE TRAINING SCHEDULE: July 1-23
(August training schedule will accompany August reference schedule)

AREA TO BE COVERED		*TIME*	
		Vogt	Kohl

Reference: During scheduled reference hours (see reference schedule):
    study the collection
    do problem sets
    form manual
    ILL-Ann Connette
    Observation of other librarians

Pauline Lilje will supervise the Reference training.

Serial Record: Check In
    Mail Sort
    Set Up
    Added Vols.

		Vogt	Kohl
Introduction:	Warren Babcock Sally Small	Mon., July 3 1-3	Mon., July 10 3-5
Check in:	Non-docs Mail Sort	Wed., July 5 1-4	Wed., July 12 1-4
Check in:	Docs Mail Sort	Thurs., July 16 8-12	Thurs., July 13 8-12
Set ups, added vols, etc. Mail sort 8-12		Fri., July 7 8-12	Fri., July 14
Orders and Collection Maintenance: Adrien Taylor		Mon., July 10 1-3	Mon., July 10 1-3
Binding: Nancy Porter, Brian Harvey		Tue., July 11 8-10	Tues., July 18 8-10
		Wed., July 12 1-3	Wed., July 19 1-3
Government Documents: Jary Anderson, Lillian Burke (Lillian will handle the U.S. Federal Depository. Jary will handle other when he returns from vacation in August)		Thur., July 13 8-12	Thur., July 20 1-4
		Fri., July 14 8-12	Fri., July 21 8-12

To Be Covered: Circulation, More time in area above, if necessary. Later, in the fall, you will be spending time in other areas of the library. In addition, you will begin participation in the general employee Orientation Program in the fall.

S.VOGT'S TRAINING SCHEDULE
24 JULY-28 JULY

SOCIAL SCIENCE CIRCULATION DESK SCHEDULE

	Sunday	Monday	Tuesday	Wednesday	Thursday	Friday	Saturday
8-9		REF					
9-10		↓	REF				
10-11			|	SER REC: SS	REF		
11-12			↓	↓	↓		
12-1							
1-2		CIRCULATION	GOV DOCS: MM	REF	CIRCULATION		
2-3		↓	↓	↓	↓		
3-4		FORMS: PL		FORMS:PL			
4-5		↓		↓			
5-6							
6-7						REF 6-10	
7-10						↓	
10-11							

DOCUMENT 3. Pauline Lilje Memorandum to Social Science Librarians. May 27, 1974, "Information for Discussion at Tuesday Meeting, May 28th, 12:00, Rm 160B."

TO: Social Science Librarians

FROM: P. Lilje

RE: Information for discussion at Tuesday meeting,
   May 28th, 12:00, Rm 160B

The current situation about Social Science Staffing needs is:

1. One faculty position (ECN's) advertised with a closing date of June 30th. The Job description expresses a preference for BA and Econ subject background. This position did not get advertised in national journals because of delays in its preparation. It was sent to library schools, etc. Hence, the applicants are mainly inexperienced new graduates. Donna McCool who had expressed an interest in this position has withdrawn.
2. Ann Connette wishes to work full time, preferably in Social Science, and Nancy Porter wishes to work part time.
3. Dr. Smith has indicated that he should be able to manipulate these two positions so that both NP's and AC's wishes can be met. This appears to be a relative certainty, not yet an accomplished fact.
4. WB's position will be vacant as of July 1. No one internally has expressed an interest in this vacancy.

In view of these developments some of our previous considerations about job responsibilities are invalid. At this time I would like to recommend the following:

- AT to be head of reference. In the event that Adrien is unable to return to work immediately reference can maintain itself. Maintaining the schedule can be someone's temporary assignment and AC can keep the material flowing.
- AC to continue with ILL's and reference collection maintenance. When Ann becomes full time she will need an additional responsibility.
- NP to continue as binding coordinator. Since Nancy has indicated that the binding as it is now organized is not a full time involvement we probably ought not to tamper with it now.
- SV to be responsible for the ordering coordination.
- JA, MF, DK, and EH are not at this time candidates for musical chairs.
- Responsibilities and activities unaccounted for, then, are: serial record, new books, college catalogs, micro materials. (I would like to see each subject specialist be responsible for initiating and maintaining files in the Vertical file that are pertinent to their subjects.)

Since we have been able to ascertain that, at least for administrative purposes, subject specialist responsibilities should consume 8-10 hours per week, or 25% of a scheduled work week, I would also like to begin working on time frames for other Divisional responsibilities. New librarians might be more comfortable with specific time frames being allotted to their assignments. (It seems to me that annual review and tenure considerations might also be more comfortable with specifics.)

To be advertised nationally the job description for our other opening should go out immediately. I think we should not state a subject preference because what we need now is a well trained, preferably experienced librarian with a general background in the social sciences. We will still be advertising for a librarian 1 or 2, if sufficiently trained and experienced. I do not think we should express a preference for someone to assume responsibility for the serial record because we box ourselves and applicants in by being that specific. Our expectation is that either one or both of the people we hire may be able to fulfill this responsibility.

Attached is the new job description which I will send on its way immediately after our meeting on Tuesday. Please be prepared with any suggested revisions. (Note: The first five paragraphs remain the same for all current library vacancies. Paragraph 6 is the only one altered, plus a rearrangement of the last sentence in paragraph 7 to emphasize serial record. The closing date is altered to enable us to advertise nationally.)

DOCUMENT 4. Organization of the Social Sciences Division Library: 1976/1977.

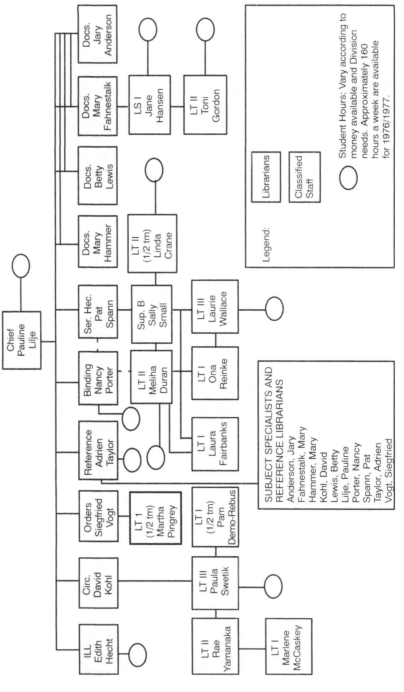

February 1, 1977

TO: Members of the Task Force on Library Administrative
Organization:

> Joselyn Druschel
> Mary Fahnestalk
> Wanda Flood
> Donna McCool
> Alice Spitzer
> Siegfried Vogt
> Keith Westover

FROM: Pauline Lilje Social Science Library

SUBJECT: Library Organization

Attached are (1) a May 21, 1976 memorandum I wrote to Dr. G. Donald Smith, Dr. Allene Schnaitter and Eleanor Kottke discussing my concerns over library organization and (2) Dr. Smith's reply of June 14, 1976. Some of you may have seen one or both of these memorandums since I routed them to all Divisions.

Upon rereading my memorandum, now almost a year old, I think the issues it raises are still cogent. Now that a Task Force on Library Administrative Organization is in existence I hope that it will deal with the issues of differentiation and centralization, as presented in my memorandum. I am furnishing copies of the memorandum and Dr. Smith's reply to all members of the Task Force in hopes that it will be useful. (The "detailed organizational charts" that are referred to are available to the Task Force for whatever purposes they might serve.)

Should you wish any other information or assistance please ask.

PL:sn
cc: Dr. Allene Schnaitter, Director of Libraries

DOCUMENT 5. Pauline Lilje Memorandum to Director, G. Donald Smith. (four pages, dated May, 1976). G. Donald Smith's Reply (two pages, dated June 14, 1976). Inclued Pauline Lilje's Cover Memorandum to the Staff. (February 1977)

TO: Dr. G. Donald Smith
    Dr. Allene Schnaitter
        Eleanor Kottke

FROM: Pauline Lilje

DATE: May 21, 1976

SUBJECT: Library organization

For over two years, since the beginning of discussions about "re-modelling" Holland Library after Science Division Library moves into its new quarters, I have been concerned, along with many others, about the effect of this move on organizational structure. The purpose of this memorandum was, at the outset, to clarify my own thinking about the organizational issues involved in 'remodelling.' It has evolved into a sort of history of organization in the Library and a discussion of what I see as the management and organizational issues involved in current activity. This memorandum does not purport to resolve these issues nor does it contain any explicit recommendations, although some of what is said carries implicit recommendations. The thrust is to urge a speedy resolution of problems that, hopefully, I spell out. The resolution of these issues has become urgent because of the imminence of the new computer systems and the development of the Washington Library Network, as legislated this spring.

When Ann Wierum and I undertook in Spring, 1975, at the request of Dr. Smith, to discuss and present plans to the Library Administrative Council for the reorganization of Holland Library, we evolved, after considerable consultation, a number of basic, possible organizational plans. These are outlined briefly below. Detailed organizational charts exist which illustrate the plans and give examples of functions and who would perform them.

1. Partial autonomous operation of all Divisions in some functions: Technical Service Division functions would continue to be handled centrally and be enlarged. A new Public Service Division would be created. It would coordinate some functions for all Divisions and some for Humanities and Social Science only. Humanities and Social Science would merge collections and some functions. The difference between this and the current organization is that the new Public Service Division would coordinate some functions currently performed in each Division.

2. Partial autonomous operation of all Divisions in all present functions: TSD functions would be handled centrally and be enlarged. The present General Public Services would be elimi-

nated. Most public service functions would be coordinated by the Library Administration Office. Social Science and Humanities would merge collections and some functions. The difference between this and number one is that LAO would coordinate some functions; there would be no public service unit as such.

3. Total autonomous operation of all Divisions in most functions: TSD functions would continue to be handled centrally. General Public Services would be eliminated and its functions handled either by the Divisions or the Library Administrative Office. Humanities and Social Science would not merge collections nor functions. This plan more or less would continue the present organization, but would clarify functions.

When Ann and I prepared the charts we hoped that an administrative decision would be made which, if not opting for any one of the plans, at least opted for some coherent organizational structure so that planning for remodelling could begin. The plans were intended to occasion discussion to such an end. All the proposals share, I believe, a commonality of treatment of organizational structural elements. That is, under any of the plans *all* Library Divisions would exercise equal degrees of autonomy over various functions, with the Director of Libraries exercising overall authority.

The organizational plan that did emerge and which currently forms the operational basis for remodelling planning is none of the above. The operational plan that evolved is ambiguous. It leaves various organizational issues unresolved and avoids dealing with incongruities. The plan was adopted as an expedient, interim and operational measure preparatory to the arrival of the new Director of Libraries who would, of course, have input into final decisions.

Subsequent to the formal adoption of this plan a remodelling committee was formed by Dr. Smith and began meeting in the fall of 1975. The committee was charged with pursuing logistic concerns only; it was not to be involved with organizational matters. It was thought that the plan adopted would suffice for remodelling purposes, that organizational niceties could be developed later when the new Director was appointed. However, since the plan only addresses primary responsibilities and does not detail how library activities are to go on, it is really only the first level of an organizational structure. Nevertheless, it was thought that the committee could proceed with logistic matters.

Apparently the organizational plan has not been sufficient. There appears to be widespread confusion about the implications, if any, of the organizational structure upon which remodelling planning is progressing. The chart is so tentative that people read into it anything they want (or don't want). It proposes coordinators, but in no way indicates what or how a coordinator is to coordinate. Organizational assumptions are being made and operated on that have never been formalized. Remodelling planning is occurring in an organizational vacuum.

The Library appears to be moving, or rather attempting to move, in two organizational directions at the same time:

1. A number of "departmentalized" functions are presumed would exist in Holland. These departments would be sub-organizational units responsible for specific functions, such as circulation and perhaps reference, and would be staffed jointly by two administratively separate Divisions which would maintain individual collection responsibilities.
2. "Divisionalized" functioning would continue in the geographically separate units. These units would apparently continue to be quite autonomous and perform all or most library operations which would be "departmentalized" in Holland.

Even if the coordinator concept would come to fruition, it is unclear what, if anything, a coordinator could meaningfully coordinate in someone else's domain. It seems we are trying to sort apples and oranges. The unplanned, "just happening" aspect of it all is extremely troublesome.

Historically (and very simplistically) the "Library" for some years now has consisted of a number of relatively autonomous organizational units called Reader Service Divisions, serviced by a centralized Technical Service Division. These Divisions are Science, Humanities, and Social Science, with the later addition of Education and Veterinary Science. Both Archives and Audio-Visual are considered to be more or less reader service divisions. Initially, in the Divisions, the thrust was that all members of the unit would perform all functions, e.g., catalogers would do reference, etc. Cataloging was the first function to go, forming the basis of TSD; other functions were left essentially in the Divisions; hence, some of the anomalous things being done in the Divisions today. For example, government documents cataloging has been shifted back and forth from TSD to Social Science twice. It is now performed in Social Science. The Library Administrative Office has always handled budgetary functions centrally under the Director's umbrella of responsibility. This organizational structure was never formalized officially within the University.

For some years Divisions were quite absolutistic in their respective autonomous behavior. Each divised its own routines, did its own book selection based on its own acquisitions policies and formulated its own policies–under the general policies umbrella of the Director. The past five to eight years have seen an effort at coordinating disparate Divisional routines into some sort of general Library policy coherence. Generally, however, this organizational structure has resulted over the years in ambiguities of implementation of centrally made policies.

The essential problem seems to be that as an organization grows in size, differentiation of tasks occurs. The structure of an organization, driven by size, almost seems to have a life of its own. It evolves in response to changing needs for control and coordination occasioned by its growth. Outside factors, such as developing technologies, affect it. Tasks divide and staff members develop expertise in performance of these tasks. Supervisors become expert in managing a particular kind of work. This expertise leads to greater efficiency because a supervisor is in charge of only one function and can supervise a larger number of subordinates than possible in a less specialized organization. In a less specialized organization, such as the small Divisions, of some years ago, duties involved the supervision of a number of different kinds of tasks and subordinates. As differentiation of tasks occurred, such as the development of General Public Services, efficiency was gained but at the expense of communication and coordination. An organization differentiating to attain the advantages of specialization must solve problems of coordination and communication. This necessitates more supervisory personnel, evident by the emergence in the Library of "function coordinators," who do this coordinating in addition to their primary responsibilities.

While management literature indicates that a broad spectrum of organizational structures exist and are effective, it still remains that the goals, missions and objectives of all organization ought to be reflected in its structure. It also should be noted that the structure of an organization determines its relationships with units outside it. It is remarked frequently in the literature today that the effectiveness of an organization can be measured by the efficiency with which it competes for scarce resources.

This differentiation of tasks and increase in size is related to the degree of centralization of the decision making process. Large size fosters decentralized decision making because of difficulties of coordinating and communication, especially when the organization has geographically separate units. A viable organization structure seems to be the result of the identification of a framework within which decisions can be reached. This the Library has not done. It has operated on a situational and sometimes personality approach to organizational structure. As it has grown in size and complexity, as problems of coordination, communication and control have arisen, it is meeting them with increasing formalization. Policies, rules, procedures are being proliferated.

There appear to be contradictory impulses at work: increase in size, complexity and differentiation are at odds with centralized decision making. Our growth has been at the expense of individual assumption of responsibility, freedom of operational judgment, and a sense of being a member of a cohesive organization. Current research tends to view organizations as open systems, indeterminate and thus able to face contingencies from without and within. This view has superseded the closed system model where organizations were presumed to react only to their own needs. Current thinking postulates, as noted above, that a measure of organizational effectiveness is how it competes for and secures the limited resources available for its functioning. And when the level of University, hence Library, funding is viewed for the coming year, this is an important postulate. During the years of the Library's growth, 1952 to the present, we lived in an era of rising expectations. A new view would seem to indicate that we will be competing, along with all other units on campus, for ever scarcer resources.

My personal preference is for an organizational structure which exhibits the greatest possibility of growth for the staff, is able to meet the exigencies of continuing budgetary crises with aplomb and composure, and for lack of a better phrase, one which leaves room to move around in. Such a structure would ideally be able to capitalize on the benefits of differentiation without sacrificing the communication and coordination benefits of autonomously functioning units. Presumably the organizational structure eventually selected for implementation will be that thought to optimize the effectiveness of performance. This is usually thought of in terms of measuring effectiveness by attainment of postulated goals, hopefully in the most humanistic way possible. The management decisions which need to be made by the Director of

Libraries in concert with the Library Administrative Council should not be postponed much longer. To further delay such decisions increases the possibility of the random development of an organizational structure characterized by lack of communication, coordination, and inability to meet demands placed on it for effective functioning.

TO: Pauline Lilje

FROM: G. D. Smith

DATE: June 14, 1976

SUBJECT: Library Organizational Structure

Your discussion of Library organizational structure raises many questions and problems. No doubt Dr. Schnaitter will undertake to define some of this as soon as she has had the opportunity to become acquainted with the Library and its people, and with the University as a whole.

I agree with you that organizational structure should be such as to further the attainment of goals and objectives. I am not sure, however, that we (I include myself in this) really understand what our goals and objectives are.

By and large, librarians are *craft* oriented–that is, with a few but relatively rare exceptions, we have been almost totally concerned with "books," the physical objects which constitute the collections. The key words of the craft are *Acquisitions* (book order, receipt, payment and accounting), *Organization* (classification and cataloging), *Preparation* (spine labels, book cards, pockets, manufacture and maintenance of card catalogs and other indexes), *Preservation* (against deterioration, destruction, loss), and *Circulation* (rules, regulations, procedures of book loan).

All of these activities are operated in accordance with more or less complex codes established outside the library by law or by interlibrary agreements such as the cataloging codes. However complex these operations are, there is very little to them that can properly be labeled "professional" as opposed to "craft" skills.

I think that most of what you call our "situational crises" to which we have reacted have occurred in these technical areas (we can hardly include the Richard Abel collapse in this category).

This leaves us with two functions which are, or should be, truly "professional": *Book Selection,* and *Information Science Service.* (I avoid deliberately the word "reference". The finding of a book or a fact in a book for a person, the referral of a person to someone or something else cannot qualify as professional service.) These two functions are oriented directly to the University curricular and research programs. Since they operate in the areas of instruction and research, they must operate as "professional" level services which receive their direction and content from those programs.

Of course, the term "professional" can be tossed around ad infinitum and ad nauseum. Everyone has his or her own definition. I think my meaning is clear however, and anyway, the definition is irrelevant to this discussion of organizational structure.

The existing organization of this library derives from my set of priorities. The first of these has been collection development. The responsibilities for "book selection" have been placed in the hands of the Area Library Chiefs and their staffs. The second priority has been to keep as many as possible of the Staff on the Reader Service floor to provide assistance to students and faculty in their use of the collections. The third has been the Technical Services which, by reason of the first two priorities have suffered from lack of centralized organization and control.

Several events of the immediate future will drastically affect the present library organization and procedures. First, you will have a new Director of Libraries in about three weeks. Dr. Schnaitter will have a different philosophy and a different set of priorities. The organization which she develops will reflect these differences.

Second, the move of Science Library to the new building away from Holland will certainly affect procedures, though probably not the priorities.

Third, the implementation of the new Automation System, scheduled to be completed during the next eighteen months, will completely revolutionize the Technical Services of this library.

For the last fifteen years or so, there has been one tremendous limitation placed upon this library's ability to perform its functions. For reasons best known to themselves, the authorities (State and Local) have restricted us to approximately 55% of staffing formula (whereas the UW Library has now reached approximately 80%). Most of our organizational and operational problems and difficulties can be traced to this overwhelming restriction.

Of necessity, we have operated on situational and personality approach to organizational requirements. Our people have had to be enormously flexible, able to adapt to the unexpected. On the whole, the "team" has done this superbly, with a minimum of obstruction and confusion.

Your new approach to organizational structure must, of course, be undertaken in this existing "situation," with all its limitations and with full comprehension of the changes which are imminent.

Personally, I do not foresee any difficulties resulting from the "departmentalization" within Holland, of which you speak. Once Science has moved out, I can see no Justification whatever for maintaining two separate Area Libraries within this building. Furthermore, with the implementation of Automation System, most of all of the activities which now constitute sections or departments within Social Sciences and Humanities–Serial Record, for example–will disappear into the computer. Circulation must be handled in this combined Area exactly as it will be handled in Science and the other Area Libraries. The projected use of subject–oriented individuals in the book selection process does not constitute departmentalization in any sense. Similarly, reference (I hate that word) may be subject oriented, but not departmentalized.

cc: E. Kottke
     A. Schnaitter

DOCUMENT 6. Allene Schnaitter, Director of Libraries to the Library Staff. Administrative Organization of the Library. (Six page plus organization chart, August 1977).

WASHINGTON STATE UNIVERSITY
PULLMAN, WASHINGTON 99163

THE LIBRARY

MEMORANDUM

TO: Library Staff

FROM: Allene Schnaitter, Director of Libraries

DATE: August 9, 1977

SUBJECT: ADMINISTRATIVE ORGANIZATION
          OF THE LIBRARY

This is a statement of the decisions I have made regarding the administrative organization of the library. It is a follow-up to the May 23 proposal developed by the Task Force on Library Administrative Organization, and the subsequent hearings and comments which I have received from many staff members and units within the library. I wish to state again my appreciation of the efforts of the many persons who participated in the process of suggesting and reviewing proposals for our future organization.

I.   *Decisions*

In general, I have accepted the proposal of the Task Force on Library Administrative Organization. Details regarding the reporting structure are as follows, and as shown on the accompanying organization chart which indicates line authority, advisory, and coordinating relationships.

Listed below, under each of the Director and Assistant Director positions are the positions or library units which report to it, plus areas the administrator coordinates.

DIRECTOR

Reporting Positions and Units

Assistant Director for Administrative Services
Assistant Director for Automation and Technical Support
Assistant Director for Public Services
Director, Audio-Visual Center (including Instructional
    Media Services)
Graphics
Head, Science & Engineering Library
Photography

Coordinates

System-wide: planning, organization, and public relations

ASSISTANT DIRECTOR FOR ADMINISTRATIVE SERVICES

Reporting Positions and Units

Head, Education Library
Head, Manuscripts, Archives, and Special Collections
Head, Veterinary Medical Library

Library Administrative Office Support Staff (excluding
secretarial support staff)

Coordinates

System-wide: budget, facilities, and personnel services

ASSISTANT DIRECTOR FOR AUTOMATION AND TECHNICAL SUPPORT

Reporting Positions and Units

Head, Technical Services
TSD Unit Heads: Acquisitions, Cataloging, searching

Coordinates

System-wide: automated services and technical processing

ASSISTANT DIRECTOR FOR PUBLIC SERVICES

Reporting Positions and Units

Holland functional units, including their system-wide coordination:

Circulation
    Collection development
    Newspapers and current periodicals
    Reference (including data base searching)
    Reserve and micro materials

Coordinates

System-wide:
    Collection development
    Library orientation
    Interlibrary loan
    Publications

II. *Basic Transitional Plans*

The persons or units listed as reporting to the new Assistant
Directors for Administrative and Public Services will begin to
report to them as soon as these Assistant Directors assume the
positions. Where there is no change in the reporting structure
from the present, the working relationships will continue. For the

units reporting directly to me, I expect to delegate (as I presently do to the Associate Director) the implementation of decisions about personnel or facilities or budget to the Assistant Director for Administrative Services.

The reporting to me of the Audio-Visual, Center Director and the units of Graphics and Photography will continue pending a final resolution, in this library and on campus, of the administrative location of these units.

When the Assistant Director for Public Services assumes his/her responsibilities, the Chiefs of Social Science and Humanities will turn over their administrative responsibilities to that person. Details about the transition are to be worked out within and between the divisions, with proposed plans reported to me. This will be fully underway as soon as our 1977-78 staffing plans are finalized.

The term "chief" to denote a division head will be discontinued, and the title "Head" will be used system-wide instead, effective with the discontinuance of the Social Science and Humanities Chiefs' responsibilities as administrators of their units.

The Associate Director of Libraries will assume a half-time position as Librarian 4, reporting to the Assistant Director of Automation and Technical Support, upon the arrival of the Assistant Director for Administrative Services. Eleanor Kottke will be in charge of special projects, primarily, at the outset, relating to remodeling plan coordination. These remodeling responsibilities will gradually be assumed, probably in one or two years, by the Assistant Director for Administrative Services. With Mrs. Kottke's assistance, I will coordinate public service concerns until the Assistant Director for Public Services arrives.

III. *Governance*

Advisory groups to make recommendations for decision-making will be organized.

To facilitate communications, the Director and three Assistant Directors will meet often, especially at the outset when the new librarians have joined the system. This will be at a scheduled time, at least twice a week, and preferably oftener. There will be no agenda, and these informal meetings will consist of day-to-day informing, conferring, and carrying out of actions which are in keeping with generally established policies and procedures relating to library administration and operations. Initially, the previous Associate Director may be present at these meetings on an invitational advisory basis, when necessary.

The Director will receive reports from, and confer with, the individual Assistant Directors when appropriate.

DIRECTOR'S COUNCIL

A group to be known as the "Director's Council" will meet on a weekly basis. This will consist of the Director, three Assistant Directors, Director of the Audio-Visual Center, and Head of the Science & Engineering Library. This group will be expected to assist the Director in making decisions regarding general library administration and operations. A prescribed agenda, including recommendations from the larger advisory Library Council, will be developed for this group.

LIBRARY COUNCIL

This ten-member group, to be known as the "Library Council" will be formed after both new Assistant Directors have arrived, and will consist of the following:

Director
  Assistant Director for Administrative Services
  Assistant Director for Automation and Technical Support
  Assistant Director for Public Services
  Director, Audio-Visual Center
  Head, Science & Engineering Library
  A representative from, and elected by, the Classified Staff, for a one-year term
  Two library faculty members, elected at large by the library faculty, from different areas of the library, for one-year terms
  Chairperson, Library Faculty Affairs Committee (the curent chair person of the LFAC will be the initial representative from this group)

This group should meet every other week, with the Director as Chairperson, with an agenda prepared in advance and distributed by the Library Administrative Office. Items for consideration may be expected to originate from the individual libraries, functional units, or individuals, or from the Director or Director's

Council. This group will function as the <u>principal advisory</u> body to the Director in the area of <u>library policy</u> formulation.

(By separate memos, I am requesting that the Classified Staff and the Library faculty elect their representatives.)

At the time that this group is established and begins to function, the Library Administrative Council, as presently constituted, will cease to function.

PUBLIC SERVICES ADMINISTRATIVE GROUP

Public service heads need to meet frequently with one another and with the Assistant Directors. For this purpose, a successor to the MiniCouncil, to be named the "'Public Service Administrative Group" is to be formed, and will consist of the Heads of the Education Library, Manuscripts, Archives, and Special Collections, Science & Engineering Library, Veterinary Medical Library, and Assistant Directors for Administrative Services and Public Services. The Director of the Audio-Visual Center will attend when topics related to AVC are on the agenda. The Director will meet with the group whenever possible.

Frequency of these meetings should be twice monthly. It is expected that this group will solve internal concerns, within and among units, will invite Technical Services personnel for matters concerning them, and will recommend items for the Library Council and Director's Council agendas.

UNIT MEETINGS WITH ASSISTANT DIRECTORS

As recommended by the Task Force on Library Administrative Organization, the Assistant Directors and Heads of the different units should be responsible for meeting with their unit heads and staffs on a regular basis.

IV. *Summary Statement*

As you readily observe, there are major changes in the offing for this library, as we plan to restructure ourselves both administratively and physically. What has been set forth in the foregoing plan is a system which has a great deal of potential for effective functioning and decision making, with considerable opportunity for communications among individuals and groups. Furthermore, no unit head is more than one administrative level away from the Director (as it is presently).

Of course, my describing the organization on paper will not make it happen. Implementation will take understanding, support and appropriate involvement on the part of the entire staff. I believe that the six principles of administration in the Task Force report take on new meaning and significance as we proceed with plans for reorganization and responsible involvement at all levels of the staff. I urge their consideration and support by all staff members. They are listed below.

I will be glad to discuss this plan further with any person or group who so wishes.

Six Principles of Administration

1. Delegation of authority at all levels is essential for the organization to function efficiently.
2. Concomitant to the principle of delegated authority is that administrators and supervisors must be accountable for their "executive" decisions.
3. Policy formulation, goal setting and planning should originate at the "grass roots" of an organization; implementation should be effected by the administrators and supervisors.
4. The span of authority, lines of authority, and areas of responsibility must be clear and unambiguous, but not so rigid as to preclude intradivisional problem recognition and recommendation.
5. Formal channels of communications, both horizontal and vertical, should be established and clearly understood by the entire staff. (Informal channels of communication, e.g., information and problem sharing, should be permitted to cross administrative lines since these may be a positive means to organizational improvements.)
6. If an organization is to be efficient and productive, authoritative (not authoritarian) and sound executive decisions are managerial imperatives; understanding, support and appropriate involvement are general staff imperatives.

[From the Task Force on Library Administrative Organization's report "PROPOSED LIBRARY ADMINISTRATIVE ORGANIZATION: EXPLANATION AND CHART" of May 23, 1977]

AFS:NW

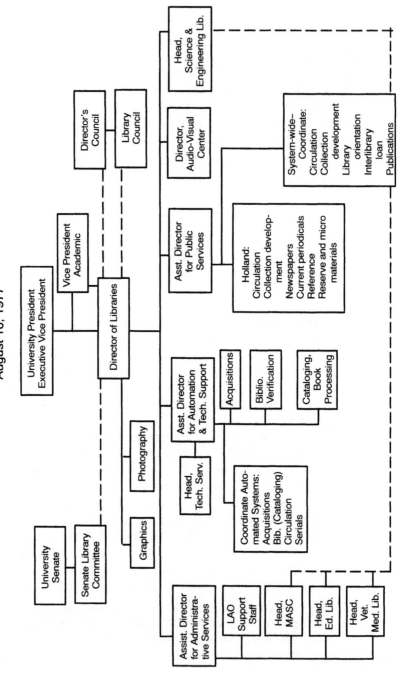

WASHINGTON STATE UNIVERSITY LIBRARIES ORGANIZATION CHART
August 10, 1977

DOCUMENT 7. Pauline Lilje Memorandum to Audrey Dibble. "Next Semester's Reference Schedule." (January, 1978)

January 30, 1978

TO: A. Dibble

FROM: P. Lilje

RE: Next semester's reference schedule

Now that there exists basic agreement on the structure of the reference schedule, it is necessary to address the issue of variability of reference hours between librarians. As I discussed with you, in Social Science it is customary for the librarians to have variable hours scheduled for reference. The reason for this is that there has been general agreement heretofore that some librarians' assignments, other than reference, were more time consuming than others. For example, the librarians in documents have customarily been regarded as having a definite commitment to not garner backlogs. There are other such examples.

Before I can do next summer's schedule it will be necessary for me to know how many hours each reference librarian will be scheduled for. Some Social Science librarians have expressed grave reservations to me about assuming more than 8 to 9 hours reference and still being able to keep up with their other assignments. Also, Dave Kohl has expressed his concerns about more than five hours reference because of the uncertain nature of staffing in the circulation unit. You may recall also that I mentioned to you that I consider 10 hours, including weekends, the minimum hours that a librarian can perform reference and maintain competency.

All of these issues combine to make it imperative that the matter be discussed immediately. Mostly, I can't do the schedule until the matter is resolved. While I believe it to be a most laudable ideal to hold the lamp of reference service high and to strive towards its light, practicality necessitates that other library work continue to proceed.

I recommend that the matter be discussed at length at the staff meeting on Wednesday. Since there is a faculty meeting that morning, perhaps Tuesday morning would be best. I.e., at the Humanities staff meeting, perhaps. At any rate, immediately.

cc: Social Science Reference Librarians

DOCUMENT 8. Pauline Lilje, Memorandum to Ron, Force, Assistant Director of Public Services. "Job Responsibilities." (September 17, 1979)

MEMORANDUM

TO: Ron Force, Assistant Director of Public Services

FROM: Pauline Lilje

DATE: September 17, 1979

SUBJECT: Job responsibilities

Below is a brief list of my current job responsibilities and hours per week to perform them. While "counting hours" is perhaps not a conceptually pure approach to accessing work loads, it seems to be the only method available to, at least, metaphorically indicate the nature and extent of job responsibilities.

RESPONSIBILITIES	ESTIMATED HOURS PER WEEK	
	Low	High
I. *Reference:* typical duties include, in addition to time scheduled, study, review, faculty and graduate student consultation, follow up time, serial record reference.	18	22
II. *Serial Record:* typical duties include administration of a nine person unit, all aspects of the serial record collection: withdraws, continuing review for cancellations, series decisions, etc. More time will likely be required for "retrospective conversion." Merging Humanities and Social Science necessitates review of many routines, in turn impacting the organization with resultant reorganization. These are time consuming administrative duties. I am developing a backlog–and the semester hasn't even begun!	15	20
III. *Subject Responsibilities:* typical duties include reading blurbs, journals and reviews in the subjects for information and book reviews, preparation of bibliographies and sources of		

information, weeding the collection, form and
book approvals, generating orders, consulting
with faculty and students, reviewing gifts for
addition to the collection, etc. (Note: there are
currently 30 book boxes of gifts from Dean
Clark's office and others in the business departments waiting for me to review. Estimated time:
20 hours.

1. Art: Western and modern: European, including
   British, Russian, Classical, Ancient Egyptian.
   Also, photography, crafts, history, criticism,
   all major and minor visual arts.   8   12
2. Department of Business Administration
3. Department of Accounting and Business Law
4. Department of Management and Administrative Systems
5. Hotel and Restaurant Management Pro-
   grams (HOSEA)   10   15

ESTIMATED HOURS PER WEEK

	Low	High
6. Environmental Studies	2	4
7. Urban and Regional Planning	2	4
8. Transportation	2	4
9. Black Studies (In Nancy Porter's absence)	2	4
10. Women's Studies (In Nancy Porter's absence)	2	4
TOTALS:	61	89

It's obvious from this brief enumeration that, even using hours
given as symbolic of missions to be accomplished, I stand little chance
of doing any one thing well. Not included in the list are activities such
as attending lectures and meetings, participation in university and
library committees, special assignments; etc. I lack time to participate
in library activities that are important and interesting to me, such as
orientation, public interest groups, the English 101 project, tours,
preparation of bibliographies, personal research, etc. Other Holland
librarians having administrative or supervisory responsibilities either
have no subject responsibilities or smaller assignments. Librarians in
Holland Public Services who have reasonable responsibilities find

time to spend on innovative and creative projects. It is frustrating, professionally demeaning and just plain unfair to be locked into a work load of such demanding proportions that I am unable to engage in activities that are professionally productive and fruitful,

There is little appreciation, acknowledgement or recognition when a librarian hauls more than a fair load, especially when its not visible, When, last spring, I agreed to become Head of Holland Serial Record it was with the expectation that my work load would not increase. It has. Part of the increase is due to the liaison responsibilities with the business departments. The College has grown much in the last two years, dividing last year into three departments comprising in total about 100 faculty members. The departments are in a state of change and growth and faculty come and go. During the last week I consulted with three new faculty, learning their subject specializations, instructing them in library procedures and generally getting to know their interests. These meetings took about five hours. I am engaged in a continuing discussion with a number of faculty concerning the purchase of some expensive SEC reports. I estimate this dialogue to take about 10 to 12 hours to resolve. All in all, I am not able to provide the services necessary to these departments and meet my other job responsibilities.

I was not formally trained in any aspect of business. I have worked to gain the necessary experience and expertise. Social Science Library tried for a number of years to hire a business subject specialist. When we were able to hire an MBA she stayed only a year, resigning for personal reasons. Before and after these fitful attempts to secure a business subject specialist, I assumed the duties. When Adrien Taylor left, Social Science librarians anticipated filling his position with a business specialist. That position was taken from Social Science.

The Library Administration wants it both ways. It offers the services of "subject specialists" to the teaching and research faculty, with a concomitant commitment implied in time and service. It then fails to provide staffing adequate to meet the demands on the librarians' time to accomplish the mission. This places the librarians in a compromised position. I no longer care to endure this discomfort.

For these reasons I request that I immediately be relieved of subject responsibilities in:

      Department of Business Administration
      Department of Accounting and Business

Department of Management and Administrative Systems
Hotel and Restaurant Management Program (HOSEA)
Environmental Studies
Urban and Regional Planning
Transportation
Black Studies
Women's Studies

I will retain Art. With the removal of these subject responsibilities I stand a chance of accomplishing my assignments more completely. There are important things to be done in various areas in art, for which I am formally trained. The photography collection needs revising and bibliographies are needed. Faculty contact in all areas is needed. I have undertaken a portrait finding aid, but have had no time to work on it. Such a portrait project might be fundable since there are few contemporary indexes. A local finding aid would be of interest to many, including the English Department.

I would appreciate a response to my request as soon as possible. I am anxious to get on with other things, I should perhaps add that, all things being equal, I consider being the business subject specialist to be a more progressive, viable professional activity that being a "supervisor." But as long as the serial record is a public service tool it will need the librarian to interface with its staff, the public, and reference librarians.

Index

Wai, Lily, 118
Washington State University Libraries.
        See also Holland Library
        (Ernest O.); Holland Library
        Public Services
    chronology, 149-55
    early online catalog systems, 36-37
    GIS services at, 126-28
    government document processing
            procedures, 114-15
    user education programs, 45-47
Webb, John, 38,127
Webmasters, 82-83
Wilder, Stanley J., 3,27
Wilkins, Walter, 14
World Civilization courses, 53-55
    assignment examples, 58-59
    collegiality and, 56-57
    early problems, 56
    growth and adaptation, 57-58
    librarian objectives, 64
    results, 61-62
    tips for teachers, 65-66
World Wide Web
    electronic resource librarians and,
            82-83
    English 101 program, 49-51
    subcommittee, 111-12

Zlatos, Christy, 6-7

For Product Safety Concerns and Information please contact our EU
representative GPSR@taylorandfrancis.com Taylor & Francis Verlag GmbH,
Kaufingerstraße 24, 80331 München, Germany

Batch number: 08153776

Printed by Printforce, the Netherlands